WITHDRAWN
FROM
COLLECTION

HEADS UP 2

Spoken English for business

Mark Tulip

with Louise Green
and Richard Nicholas

DELTA
PUBLISHING

DELTA Publishing
Quince Cottage
Hoe Lane
Peaslake
Surrey GU5 9SW
England

www.deltapublishing.co.uk

© DELTA Publishing 2015

All rights reserved. No reproduction, copy or transmission of this publication may be made without written permission from the publishers or in accordance with the provisions of the Copyright, Designs and Patents Act 1988, or under the terms of any licence permitting copying issued by the Copyright Licensing Agency, Saffron House, 6–10 Kirby Street, London EC1N 8TS.

First published 2015

Edited by Catriona Watson-Brown
Designed by Greg Sweetnam
Cover design by Greg Sweetnam
Printed by RR Donnelley in China

ISBN 978-1-905085-97-2

Photo acknowledgements
Alamy: pages 34 (4), 40 (top), 76 (top)
Automattic: page 34 (logo)
Cartoonstock: pages 30, 53
Corbis: page 68 (bottom)
Elliott Erwitt / Magnum Photos: page 44 (top)
Getty: page 6 (Ex 1)
Lush Cosmetics: page 76 (logo)
Shutterstock: pages 4, 5, 6 (Ex 3 top left, top middle, bottom left, bottom middle), 8, 9, 10, 11, 12, 13, 14, 16, 18, 20 (bottom), 24, 26, 28, 32, 33, 34 (1 and 3), 36, 37, 38, 40 (bottom), 41, 44 (bottom), 46, 48, 49, 50, 52, 56, 58, 59, 60, 61, 64, 65, 66 (1, 4, 5), 68 (top), 70, 72 (1, 3, 4, 5, 6, 7, 8, 9, 10, 11, 12), 74, 79, 80, 81, 82, 85
Thinkstock: page 6 (Ex 3 top right, bottom right), 15, 34 (2), 66 (3), 72 (2)
Weinstein Company/UK Film Council/See Saw Films/The Kobal Collection: page 20 (top)

Illustration acknowledgements
Oxford Designers and Illustrators Ltd: pages 36, 66 (bottom right); Mike Philips, Beehive Illustration: page 22; Vince Reid, Beehive Illustration: pages 62, 74; Rory Walker: pages 54–55

Text acknowledgements
We are grateful to the following for permission to reproduce copyright material: US Department of Labor and the US Department of Labor Statistics for US consumer spend statistics, an April 2009. Source: Department of Labor; Cengage Learning for a figure from *Audio-visual methods in Teaching* by Edgar Dale, p.107, Drydon Press, 1946, 1954, 1969. Reproduced by permission of Copyright Clearance Center; IKEA for statistics from *2013 Facts & Figures*, Sept 2012–August 2013, pp.4–5. Used with permission from Inter IKEA Systems B.V. 2014; Statistic Brain Research Institute for FedEx Company Statistics – Statistic Brain, 2014 Statistic Brain Research Institute, publishing as Statistic Brain. RESEARCH DATE 11.12.2002, http://www.statisticbrain.com/fedex-company-statistics/; and IEA Statistics for the figure 'Top ten countries for CO_2 emissions from fuel combustion (2012)' from CO_2 Emissions from Fuel Combustion Highlights, 2014, http://www.iea.org/publications/freepublications/publication/CO2EmissionsFromFuelCombustionHighlights2014.pdf, p.11, IEA Publishing, copyright © OECD/IEA Statistics, Licence: http://www.iea.org/t&c/termsandconditions/.

Contents

My curriculum vitae

Talk about your background and experience

1 CVs, or resumés, can vary from country to country. Which of the following do you have on your CV? Why?

> photo   age   marital status   e-mail address   Facebook address   LinkedIn address   Twitter address   education   qualifications   work experience   languages   courses   key skills   interests   references   why you left your last job   Skype address

*In North America, job applicants usually send a resumé, while in the rest of the English-speaking world, a CV is preferred. A resumé is usually shorter than a CV and more targeted at a particular job.

Listening

2 (((1.1))) Peter Carson is interested in the job advertised below. You're going to hear a phone call between Peter and Tina Fowler at Telstram Ltd. Read Peter's CV below, then listen and find three mistakes in the CV.

TELSTRAM LTD

Position: Sales Executive, British Columbia, Canada
Job code: TE002
Experience: 3–5 years
Graduates (Marketing) with experience in product selling (IT).
The role includes negotiating commercial agreements, public relations, identifying new home and European markets and business opportunities, communicating with target audiences and managing customer relationships.
Contact: Tina Fowler
Tel: 0181 3438466
E-mail: tfowler@telstram.com

---

3 (((1.1))) Read the Key language for talking about your CV on page 5, then listen again and tick (✓) the expressions you hear.

Peter Carson
1086 South Pender St, Vancouver
V8B 23L Canada
Home telephone: 0181 3938104
Cell: 09435 683957
E-mail: p.carson@wb.net

KEY SKILLS
- excellent sales record
- IT, including advanced knowledge of Java and MS Office
- good German
- highly skilled presenter and negotiator

EDUCATION
BSc Computer Studies (University of Toronto, 2005)

WORK EXPERIENCE

Dates	Position and location
2011–now	Area Sales Representative, PTK Foods, Canada
2006–2011	Sales Representative, Orax Corp, England (one year in Paris)

COURSES
Java Programming 2010

INTERESTS
Tennis, hiking

REFERENCES
On request

Key language for talking about your CV

I was born in [place] on [date].
I have / I've got a degree / Bachelor's degree / Master's degree / diploma in [subject] from [place].
I'm qualified as a [job title].
I've trained to be a [job title].
I worked for [company] from [year] to [year].
I've (only) been working for [company] for [time period] / since [point of time].
I'm currently working as a [job title] for [company] on [project/temporary activity].
I have experience in [area of work].
I've done training courses in [subject area].
I'm very keen on / interested in [topic].

Get ready

4 **Think of the questions you'd need to ask in order to get the information in the Key language section.**

Examples:
What professional qualifications do you have?
Can you tell me about your work experience?

Pronunciation   Linking 1: consonant + vowel

1 **When a word finishes with a consonant sound and the next word starts with a vowel, there is a link between them. Mark the links as in the example.**

1 I was born‿in Paris.
2 He's qualified as an engineer.
3 She's got a degree in economics.
4 He resigned on Friday.
5 I'm currently working as a flight attendant.
6 She went out at eight.
7 He sent in his CV to the company.

2 ((1.2)) **Listen, check and repeat the sentences.**

Task

5 **Use the questions you prepared in Exercise 4 to interview other students or your teacher about their CVs.**

Follow-up

6 **Discuss these questions.**

1 Do you agree that it's always better to go to university rather than go straight into work when you leave school?
2 How has communications technology changed the way we apply for jobs?
3 Do you think a higher salary should be your top priority when looking for a new job?
4 What should you say in your covering e-mail?
5 Would you say it's better to get experience in lots of jobs, or try to develop your career in just one or two places?

02 My job description

In 2009, Ben Southall beat 34,000 other candidates for 'The Best Job in the World': the caretaker on a tropical Australian island, with a A$150,000 salary, a beachside villa and a private swimming pool. But after he started his dream job, Ben had second thoughts. He had to work seven days a week and up to 19 hours a day on a schedule of promotional events, press conferences and administrative duties.

1 Discuss these questions.

1 Would you like the job described above?
2 What's your job title?
3 How long have you had this job?
4 What did you do before?
5 Do you enjoy your work? Why? / Why not?
6 What would be your ideal job?

Listening

2 (((2.1))) **You're going to hear three of the six business people in the photos describing their main responsibilities at work. Who is talking in each case (1–3)?**

IT Analyst

Executive Assistant

Factory Manager

Finance Manager

Organisation Analyst

HR Manager

3 (((2.1))) **Look at the Key language and listen again. Tick (✓) the expressions the speakers use.**

Key language for describing your job

The main purpose of my job is to …
The main thing I do is …
This involves (–ing)
Another important part of my job is …
I have to deal with / see to / take care of …
I'm responsible for / in charge of …
It's my job to / I have to / I've got to …
I manage/run/organise …

Pronunciation Common mistakes

1 How do you pronounce the words in bold in these sentences?

1 She has to hire more **personnel**.
2 What's the main **purpose** of your job?
3 I have to deal with problems that come up every day, **although** I don't always manage to solve them.
4 This involves working with three other **colleagues**.
5 It's my job to **analyse** other people's jobs.
6 I've got to write an **analysis** of his job.
7 He said he's bought a new **suit**.
8 The company has more than two thousand **employees** worldwide.

2 (((2.2))) **Listen to and repeat the sentences.**

Get ready

4 If a verb follows a preposition, the –ing form is used (e.g. *He's in charge of buying*). Choose the correct form of the verb in each of these sentences.

1 I have to *prepare / preparing* presentations.
2 I'm also responsible for *co-ordinate / co-ordinating* other people.
3 The main purpose of my job is to *improve / improving* the effectiveness of our machinery on the production line.
4 I take care of *answer / answering* customers' queries.
5 In my job, I've got to *liaise / liaising* with the HR department.
6 I look forward to *see / seeing* you at the interview.

5 Work with a partner. Think of somebody you know who does a different job to you. Ask each other the questions below and use the Key language to answer.

What do they do?
What's the main purpose of their job?
What does the job involve?
What else do they have to do in the job?
Are they in charge of other people? Who?

Task

6 Make brief notes about your tasks at work, then talk about them in more detail. Where necessary, describe sub-tasks too (see example below).

Main tasks	Sub-tasks
hiring personnel	*consulting with departments, shortlisting candidates, arranging interviews*

Follow-up

7 Discuss these questions.

1 What is the purpose of job descriptions?
2 Are job descriptions clearly defined in your organisation?
3 Which parts of your job do you think are the most important? And the least important?
4 Which part of your work takes up most of your time?
5 Which part of your job do you like most? Why?
6 Does your job description really describe what you do?
7 Do you think you have too much to do at work? If so, what would be the best solution to this?

03 Away on business

Use the language of travel

I love going away on business. I can see new places, and it can be a great networking opportunity.

Transport delays, boring hotel rooms, evenings with people you don't want to be with ... No, no – video conferencing's the way to do it.

1 Look at the people above and answer these questions.

1 Who do you agree with? Why?

2 Have you travelled much on business? Do you think you'll travel more in the future?

Listening

2 (((3.1))) **Anna Rossi is a brand manager with a multinational. She's been on a short course in London, but is now back in Milan and talking with Ric, a colleague from the marketing department. Follow her route on the plan below and choose the correct alternative at each stage (1–8).**

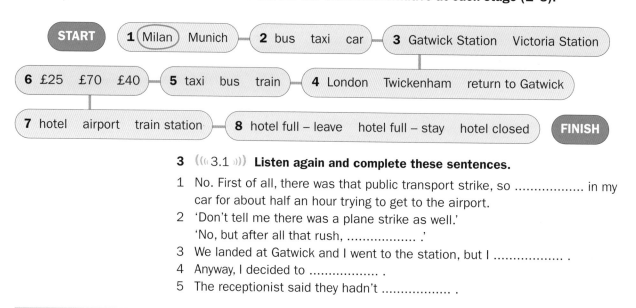

START
1 Milan   Munich
2 bus   taxi   car
3 Gatwick Station   Victoria Station

6 £25   £70   £40
5 taxi   bus   train
4 London   Twickenham   return to Gatwick

7 hotel   airport   train station
8 hotel full – leave   hotel full – stay   hotel closed
FINISH

3 (((3.1))) **Listen again and complete these sentences.**

1 No. First of all, there was that public transport strike, so .... in my car for about half an hour trying to get to the airport.

2 'Don't tell me there was a plane strike as well.'
'No, but after all that rush, ...'

3 We landed at Gatwick and I went to the station, but I ....

4 Anyway, I decided to ....

5 The receptionist said they hadn't ....

Key language for travelling

to arrive **in** [a country/town]
to arrive **at** [other places]
to travel (not a travel)

to get a connecting flight

to stay in a hotel
to get stuck in traffic / in a traffic jam
to get/take/catch a train/bus, etc.
to miss a bus/train, etc.

Phrasal verbs for travel
to **get on/off** a train/bus/plane/bike, etc.
to **get into / out of** a car

How long does it take (you) **to get to** ... ?
It takes (me) ...
to **set off on** a trip/journey
to be delayed / **held up** in traffic
to land / **take off**
to **pick somebody up / drop somebody off** at the airport
to **check into / out of** a hotel

4 Use the correct form of phrasal verbs of travel from the Key language section to complete these sentences.

1 My train should arrive at half past one. Could you .... me .... at the station?
2 The plane .... from Moscow Domodedovo Airport at 15:30 yesterday.
3 We .... on our trip to Helsinki early in the morning.
4 I was .... in traffic when I was trying to get to the airport.
5 When I arrived in Shanghai, I .... to the Pudong Hotel.
6 When the meeting finished, the company car .... me .... at the airport.

5 Look again at the plan in Exercise 2 and use the Key language to describe Anna's journey.

Pronunciation –ed endings

1 (((3.2))) **Listen to 18 verbs ending in –ed. How many syllables are there in each verb: one, two or three?**

2 (((3.2))) **Listen again and put the verbs into three groups, according to the sound of their –ed endings.**

/t/	/d/	/ɪd/

3 Use the verbs to make simple sentences and practise saying them to your partner.

---

6 Ask your partner about a business or leisure trip they've been on. You can use these prompts.

where / go? / why?
can / describe / journey?
how long / take / get there?
delayed? / why?
what time / arrive?
where / stay?
who / meet?
what / talk about / discuss?
what / do there?
visit / anywhere in particular?
what / food like?
what / weather like?
any problems? / what?
how much / spend?
who / paid?
like / go there again?

7 Have you ever had a very difficult journey? What happened?

04 Personal finance

Use the language of everyday personal finance

Compare your budget with others

1 Say to what degree you agree with these sentences.

Always spend less than you earn.
Don't wait until you're older than 25 before starting to save for a pension.
The best way to pay off a credit card is by using another credit card.
Always save at least 5% of what you earn.
Never lend or borrow money.
Online banking isn't safe.
The best things in life are free.

> Yes, absolutely.

> Yes, I agree up to a point, but …

> That depends on …

> I don't agree at all.

Listening

2 (((4.1))) Alex and Pilar Gallo live in Melbourne, Australia. They own a small business and need to carefully control their finances. Try to guess the correct answers (a, b or c) to these questions. Then listen and check.

1 Alex and his wife owe .... on their house.
   a $200,000   **b** $1,400   **c** $130,000
2 They usually spend .... $200 a week in the supermarket.
   a more than   **b** less than   **c** exactly
3 They have to pay their daughter's university ....
   a fees   **b** taxes   **c** bills
4 They sometimes lend a car to ....
   a neighbours   **b** friends   **c** others in their family
5 They manage to save .... at the end of the month.
   a nothing   **b** a lot   **c** a little
6 With the profits from their company, they ....
   a give themselves a rise   **b** reinvest in their company   **c** save for pensions

---

Key language for personal finance

Expressions with *pay*

to pay
- somebody for something
- income tax
- a bill
- back/off a debt / a loan / a mortgage
- by credit card / debit card
- (in) cash
- rent
- interest
- a fine
- fees

Verbs of personal finance

to earn a salary (*monthly*) / wages (*weekly*)
to get a rise (BrE) / a raise (AmE) / a bonus
to save for a pension
to be able to afford something
to borrow money from
to lend somebody money
to owe somebody money
to own property / real estate
to spend your income on something

Get ready

3 Complete these sentences using expressions with *pay* from the Key language section.

1 At the end of the meal, we paid the .... and left.
2 We're paying .... a mortgage of €100,000. The house will be ours after 15 years.
3 I don't own this flat, I pay .... of €800 a month.
4 The customer didn't have any cash, so she paid ....
5 We paid the electrician .... the work he'd done in the kitchen.
6 The book was only €9, so I paid in ....

The loan shark

4 Complete this text with verbs of personal finance from the Key language section.

Borrowing money

Many people will be happy to [1]................. you money, but if you do not [2]................. a high enough salary from your job to pay back the money you [3]................. from them on time, then you can quickly find yourself in trouble. The lenders can even take the things you [4]................. , like your house or car, in payment. Never [5]................. more money than you can [6]................. to pay back.

Pronunciation   The *r* sound

1 (((4.2))) **Listen and repeat.**

right married
To make this *r* sound, push your lips out a little, curl the top of your tongue back but don't touch the roof of your mouth.

2 (((4.3))) **Listen and repeat the words you hear.**

Task

5 Look at the annual spending of an average American family. Talk to your partner. Go through the expense items and compare the Americans' spending with yours.

- What do you spend a greater percentage of your income on?
- What do you spend less on?
- What do you spend about the same on?

Average family unit = 2.5 people, including two adults aged 48 Gross income average: $49,639		
Transport	$8,758	17.6%
Housing including utilities, furniture, etc.	$16,920	34.1%
Healthcare	$2,853	5.7%
Personal care	$588	1.2%
Reading	$118	0.2%
Clothes	$1,881	3.8%
Education	$945	1.9%
Insurance, pensions	$5,336	10.8%
Entertainment	$2,698	5.4%
Food	$6,133	12.4%
Alcohol	$457	0.9%
Tobacco	$323	0.7%
Miscellaneous	$2,629	5.3%

source: US Department of Labor 2009

Follow-up

6 Discuss these questions.

- Are you good at saving? Why? / Why not?
- What do you think you spend too much on? Why?
- Do you think it will be easier to save in the future?
- What would you like to buy if you could afford it?
- If someone gave you US$200,000, would you just keep it in the bank? Why? / Why not?

Problems and solutions

Use the language of problem-solving

1 An important client is 30 days late in paying a large invoice. Which of the following would you do, and in what order?

- Offer the client a discount if they pay within a week. ☐
- Draw up a new contract to be used in the future with this client, with penalty clauses for late payment. ☐
- Draw up a new contract to be used in the future with this client, with discounts for prompt payment. ☐
- Call the client and ask why they haven't paid. ☐
- Send a letter to the client threatening legal action. ☐
- Say nothing and take out a bank loan if necessary. ☐
- Send the client another reminder of the debt. ☐
- Insist on a meeting with the client. ☐

2 Have you ever been in a difficult situation like the one above? What did you do?

Listening

3 (((5.1))) Listen to an interview in which analyst Maxine Binnie explains the 'five whys' approach to problem-solving. What is this technique?

4 (((5.1))) Listen again and answer these questions.

1 Why are sales down?
2 Why have their prices increased?
3 Why have their costs increased?
4 Why do they only buy their supplies from the USA?
5 Why haven't they looked for other suppliers who could offer the same at a lower price?

Key language for problem-solving

Giving reasons
Customers don't buy it **because** it's too expensive.
They don't buy it **because of** the high price.
The reason why they don't buy it is the high price.

Giving results
Since/As the price is too high, they don't buy it.
The price is too high, **so / consequently / as a result** they don't buy it.

Offering solutions
Why don't you …?
You should / ought to …
You could … by (–ing)
What about (–ing)?
I suggest (–ing)
I recommend (–ing)

---

5 Work with a partner.

Student A: Read your problem (see below) to Student B who should respond with *why* questions to each answer. Use the language for giving reasons and results from the Key language section to answer Student B's questions.

Examples:

A: *Our products are good, but we don't have enough customers.*

B: *Why don't you have enough customers?*

A: *We don't have enough customers because the potential customers don't know about the products.*

Student A: Problem

Your products are good, but you don't have enough customers.

Why? → Potential customers don't know about the products.

Why? → There is very little marketing.

Why? → There is a very small budget for marketing.

Why? → Some people in the company don't think that marketing is very important.

Student B: Use the language for offering solutions from the Key language section to suggest some advice to Student A about their problem.

6 Repeat Exercise 5 for Student B's problem.

Student B: Problem

One of the machine operators in your factory has had an accident with the machine he was operating.

Why? → He didn't follow the safety procedures.

Why? → He wasn't trained to use the machine.

Why? → He had replaced the usual operator who was absent.

Why? → The procedure for replacing absentees isn't planned well enough.

Pronunciation Contractions
1 (((5.2))) **Contractions are commonly used in fluent spoken English. Listen to six sentences and write the contraction you hear in each one.**   Example: 1 *don't*   **2** (((5.2))) **Listen again and repeat the sentences.**

Task

7 List some problems you have at work. Then talk to a colleague to describe the problems, identify the causes and discuss solutions.

06 Socialising 1

Order and pay for food in a restaurant

1 Look at the menu below. Which of these categories would you put each food item in?

Vegetable	Fruit	Meat	Fish/Seafood	Other
aubergine				

ECRO'S

MENU

Starters

Baked aubergine stuffed with cheese and walnuts

Leek and potato soup

Mackerel on toast with cucumber and radish

Roasted figs in Parma ham with blue cheese and rocket

Main course

Grilled fillet of sea bass with artichokes, tomato, olives and aubergine

Roast pork stuffed with apple and cranberries

Baked cod with lemon and butter sauce

Stir-fried beef, broccoli and garlic

Chicken and dumplings in a vegetable stew

Chickpea and potato curry

Prawns with egg-fried rice and peas

Liver and onions with mashed potato

Breast of duck with blackcurrants

Summer salad: mushrooms, beans, tomatoes, lettuce and parmesan

Dessert

Apricot soufflé with chocolate sauce

Apple and blackberry pie with cream

Fruit salad: melon, pineapple, grapes, kiwi, grapefruit

Rhubarb crumble with ice cream

Raspberry cheesecake

Drinks

A selection of red, white and rosé wines

Fresh fruit juices

Still/sparkling mineral water

Listening

2 (((6.1))) Listen to the conversation between a waiter and customers at Ecro's Restaurant and complete the customers' orders on the waiter's notepad.

Table 8

Starters

Main courses

Desserts

Drinks

3 Which topic in this 'Conversation menu' did the customers talk about at the end of audio 6.1?

CONVERSATION MENU

- the restaurant
- the waiter
- vegetarians
- cooking
- drinks
- tipping in restaurants
- the weather
- the news
- modern technology

- shopping
- business
- travel
- cars and driving
- country comparisons
- future plans
- art and architecture
- sport
- holidays

Key language for a restaurant

Arriving

There are four of us. / A table for four, please.
Do you have a table for two? We don't have a reservation.

At the table

Excuse me! (*to call the waiter*)
Could we see the menu / wine list, please?
What would you recommend?
I'll have / I'd like …
The same for me, please.

Paying

Could we have the bill, please?
Can I pay by credit card?

Complaining

I'm sorry, but this is cold / not cooked, etc.
I asked for … , but …
Will it take much longer?
This doesn't taste right.

Starting conversations

What do you think of …?
Have you heard about …?
Do you like …?
Have you seen …?
Have you ever been to …?

Pronunciation *th*

1 Write these words in the correct column of the table below, according to whether they have the voiced /ð/ sound or the unvoiced /θ/ sound.

although both clothes healthy mouth other something teeth thank that the then there thing think together

/ð/ **voiced**	/θ/ **unvoiced**
although	*both*

2 (((6.2))) Listen and check your answers. Then practise saying the words.

Task

4 You're in Ecro's restaurant with your partner. Your teacher is the waiter/waitress. Choose and order your meal from the menu on page 14.

5 What are you going to talk about during your meal? Choose your own topics or choose from the 'Conversation menu' in Exercise 3. You can use the *Starting conversations* expressions in the Key language section.

07 My phone calls

Make and receive phone calls

A mobile phone

B Skype

C audio conference call

1 Match these sentences with the types of calls in the photos above. Explain your choices.

1 You should have an agenda and a list of the participants in front of you before this type of call.
2 You can see who you're talking to, but there can be problems if the connection's slow.
3 It's best not to make an important call in a public place with this.
4 It's necessary to arrange this kind of call in advance.
5 This is the most difficult to understand.

2 Which type of call do you prefer? Why?

Listening

3 (((7.1))) **Listen and correct the phone messages.**

❶

GT Zurich called about accommodation at the conference.
  They've changed your hotel from the Marriott Hotel to the Rex in Talstrasse.
  OK?

❷

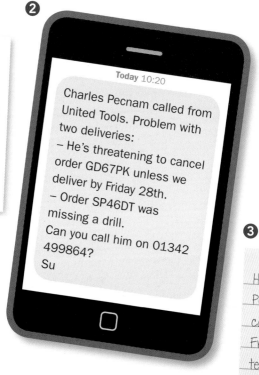

Today 10:20

Charles Pecnam called from United Tools. Problem with two deliveries:
– He's threatening to cancel order GD67PK unless we deliver by Friday 28th.
– Order SP46DT was missing a drill.
Can you call him on 01342 499864?
Su

❸

Hi Phoebe,
Portslade Mechanics called about your car. They say it won't be ready till Friday. It'll cost about £100.
tel: 01554 623090
e-mail: portmeck@freestyle.co.uk
Emily

Key language for telephoning

Caller	Call receiver
Starting the call Good morning, this is Petra Skov from CDT. Hello, it's Petra Skov from CDT here.	**Answering the call** Good morning/afternoon, Newtech Export.
Saying who you want I'd like to speak to ...., please. Could / May I speak to ...., please?	**Passing the call** Hold on / Hold the line, please, I'll connect you. (*in another office*) Yes, I'll pass you to him/her. (*in the same office*) Speaking! (*if the person asked for is you*)
Explaining the reason for your call I'm calling about the meeting on Friday. I'm calling to ask ...	**Saying somebody is not available** I'm sorry, he's/she's not in at the moment. I'm afraid he's/she's away in Poland until Friday.
Leaving a message Can I leave a message? Could you ask him/her to call me back?	**Offering to take a message** Can I take a message? If you give me your number, I'll ask him/her to call you back later.
Leaving contact information She can call me on 01273 747343.	**Asking for repetition** Sorry, could you say that again, please? Sorry, I didn't catch your name.
Finishing the call Right, I think that's all. I look forward to seeing you on Friday. Was there anything else?	

Get ready

4 Work with a partner. Take it in turns to practise both sides of this conversation.

A You're at work at KTP plc. Somebody calls to speak to your boss, Mr Luc. Answer the phone.

B Start the call. You want to speak to Mr Luc.

B Explain the reason for your call. You're preparing a contract with KTP. There's a problem with it. You need to speak to Mr Luc. Give your contact details.

A Your boss has gone to another town today for a meeting. Offer to take a message.

A Take the message and ask for repetition of contact details.

A Finish the call.

B Finish the call.

A Say Mr Luc will call back later today.

B Answer.

5 Prepare and role-play the conversation between Mr Luc and Speaker B from Exercise 4.

Mr Luc: Say why you're calling.

Speaker B: Explain the problem: the contract states that KTP will deliver the goods by 12th June. You need to make this earlier: 15th May.

Task

6 Work with a partner. Make and receive examples of calls from your work.

1 Make a short list of possible calls. For each call, decide who's calling who, and why.

2 Prepare to make the calls with a partner.

3 Take it in turns to make and receive the calls.

08 My presentations 1

Present information

1 The diagram on the right shows how people remember things best (i.e. they remember more from the activities at the bottom than those at the top). What can this tell us about giving presentations?

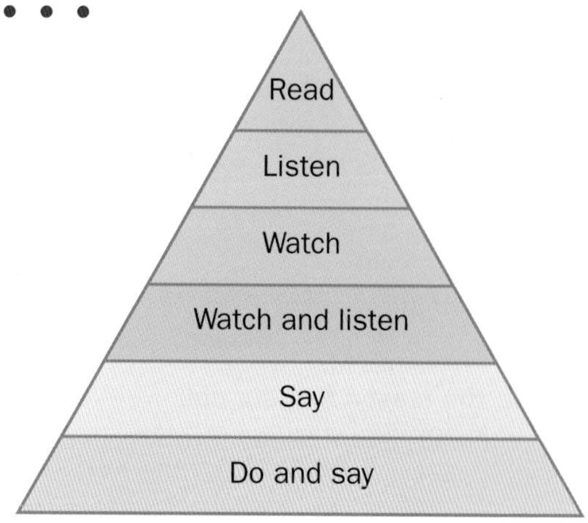
Read
Listen
Watch
Watch and listen
Say
Do and say

Dale's Pyramid of Learning

Listening

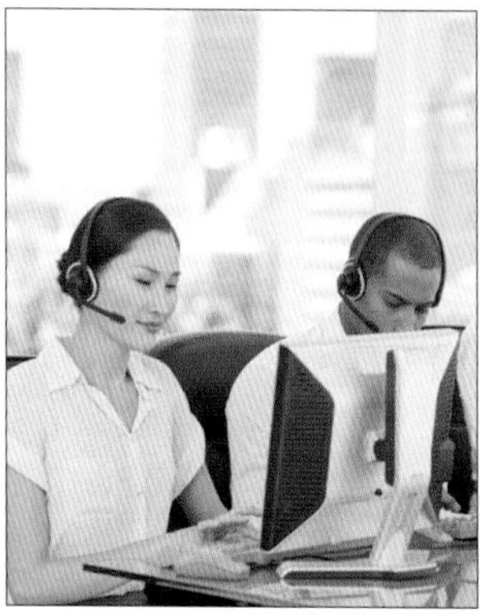

2 (((8.1))) **Suchin Bak is an airline Customer Services Manager. Listen to her explaining the procedure for handling customer complaints to a group of new employees. Decide if these sentences are true (T) or false (F). Correct the false ones.**

1 The subject of the presentation is complaints to the airline by phone.
2 In the second part of the presentation, Suchin talks about how to deal with complaints.
3 The company has strict rules on how to respond to customers.
4 In the last part, the participants work on their own to practise dealing with complaints.

3 (((8.1))) **Look at the Key kanguage for presenting information on page 19, then listen again and tick (✓) the ones you hear.**

Get ready

4 Work with a partner.

Student A: Use the Key language to practise giving a short presentation of information about the company below.
Student B: Do the same with the information on page 85.

Student A

IKEA

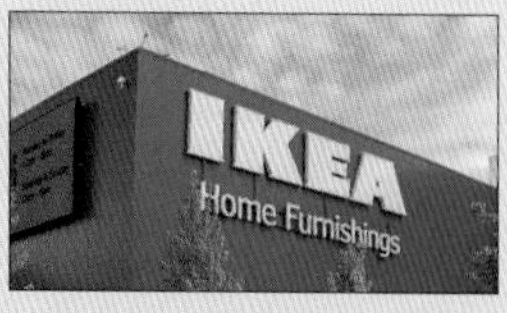
IKEA
Home Furnishings

Background
Swedish entrepreneur Ingvar Kamprad developed IKEA in the 1940s and 50s.
Keys to success: design, self-assembly, advertising, catalogue, showroom

The stores

Number of IKEA stores worldwide:	345
Number of countries that have an IKEA store:	42

The customers

IKEA store visits:	775 million
IKEA catalogue application downloads:	9.7 million
IKEA website visits:	1.2 billion
Total number of BILLY bookcases sold worldwide:	41 million

Finance

IKEA sales turnover:	29.2 billion euros

All figures are for 2012–2013.

Key language for presenting information

Presenting the subject

I'm going to talk about / present / describe / explain …

The purpose of this talk today / this morning is to …

Questions

If you have any questions, please feel free to interrupt.

I'll be glad to answer any questions you may have at the end of my talk.

Providing background information

First of all, let me give you some background information on this product.

I'll start with some general information on …

Informing

The main points we'll **look at** today are …

I'll **outline** the main reasons for this.

I should **clarify** this.

I'd like to **point out** …

I can **update you** / **give you an update** on the situation.

Referring to slides

As you can see here / from this diagram, …

Have a look at …

This chart illustrates/describes …

Underlining points

You'll notice that …

It's important to remember that …

This is important/significant because …

I must emphasise that …

Moving on

We've seen …; now let's move/go on to …

Now we come to … / That now brings us to … / Let's turn now to …

Finally, …

Ending

I hope that's given you a clear idea/picture of …

That brings me to the end of the presentation.

Thank you. Are there any (more) questions?

Pronunciation   Contrast stress

We can stress words to show contrast or to disagree or correct.

1 (((8.2))) **Listen and underline the words stressed for contrast.**

1 These are not suggestions for steps, they are the only way you are allowed to answer.

2 I don't want to lower some of our prices, I want to lower all of our prices.

3 As you can see from the graph, sales didn't go down in June, they went up.

2 Practise saying the sentences in Pronunciation Exercise 1.

3 (((8.3))) **Listen and underline the words stressed by Speaker B.**

1 **A** James has gone to Detroit.
  B No, he hasn't gone to Detroit, he's gone to Chicago.

2 **A** Did you call on Wednesday or Thursday?
  B I called on Wednesday and Thursday.

3 **A** You haven't finished the report.
  B I have finished the report.

4 Practise saying the dialogues in Pronunciation Exercise 3 with a partner.

Task

5 **Prepare to give a presentation in which you provide information about an aspect of your work or about your company as a whole. Give your presentation a clear structure and use visual aids where possible.**

Follow-up

6 **Give each other feedback on your presentations. What was good about them? What could be improved?**

My presentations 2

Propose and persuade

1 Read the pieces of advice below about giving presentations and decide how useful you think each one is.

	Good advice	It depends	Bad advice
1 Learn as much as possible about your audience before you begin.			
2 Don't use PowerPoint. It's just slide after slide of bullet points read out by the presenter.			
3 Get the audience emotionally engaged. Look them in the eye, tell stories, show pictures, be enthusiastic.			
4 Never speak for longer than the time allotted to you.			
5 Use as many types of media and as much colour as possible.			
6 While speaking, look at a member of the audience for a few seconds, then move to another person and do the same.			
7 Drink lots of water.			
8 Keep smiling.			
9 Never apologise.			

Listening

2 You're going to hear part of a meeting involving Kurt Wenders, a senior executive in the construction company JLB Gmbh. Business has been very difficult for them recently, and Kurt needs to ask the board of directors for radical changes to turn the company around. Before you listen, look at these three possible causes of JLB's problems.

a The competition is too strong.
b The bank is putting too much pressure on them.
c The company has too many assets which they aren't using.

3 (((9.1))) Listen and decide which possible cause (a, b or c) Kurt identifies in particular.

4 (((9.1))) Read the Key language on page 21, then listen again and tick (✓) the phrases you hear.

Key language for presenting in order to propose and persuade

Focusing

I would underline/highlight …
Let's look at this in more detail.
In particular, …
What does that mean for us?

Stating objectives

What we've got to do is …
Our main aim/objective must be to …
We must do something about …

Making proposals

I suggest/recommend (doing)
I suggest/recommend we/you (do)
I strongly suggest …

Persuading

I'm sure you all agree that …
In my experience, …
From the evidence, it certainly appears that …
It certainly seems that …
It makes sense to …
Obviously/Clearly, …
There can only be one conclusion: …

Arguing for change

Strong
It doesn't make sense.
What's the point?
It's pointless.

Milder
I think we can improve on this.
I think it would be better to …

Pronunciation	Sentence stress

1 **Stress on words depends on the information that the speaker wants to show is important. Read the highlighted section of audio script 9.1 on page 89 and underline the words you think should be stressed.**

2 (((9.1))) **Listen again and compare your answers.**

3 **Work with a partner. Read the extract to each other, using the same sentence stress.**

Task

5 **Prepare a presentation, using the Key language to help you make a proposal. Choose your own topic or one of the following:**

- why customers should choose your product or service
- how to improve customer relationships
- how to cut costs
- how to improve staff morale

Tips

- Give your presentation a clear structure (see Unit 8).
- Explain the background to your ideas.
- Present strong reasons in favour of your proposal, underlining the benefits.
- Provide specific, practical examples.
- Involve the audience where possible.

Follow-up

6 **Give each other feedback on your presentations. What was good about them? What wasn't? How could they be improved?**

10 Socialising 2

1 These people are meeting at a break in a conference. What's going wrong?

What do you think?

Are you going to the talk on new technologies?

How long have you been at the conference?

What do I think about what?

No.

Should I say 'I'm here for two days' or 'I've been here for two days'? Mmm, I'll probably make a mistake …

Key language for making good conversation 1

Asking open questions

What did you do at the weekend?
Where did you go?
Who did you meet?
Why did you go to (Nerja)?
When did you leave?
How did you get there?

Showing interest

Oh, yes? / Oh yeah?
Really?
Are you? / Do you?, etc.

Identifying things you have in common

Me too.
Me neither.

Asking follow-up questions

A I won a prize in the competition.
B Really? What did you win?

Agreeing by reforming the comment

A We had a good time at the party.
B Yeah, it was fun.

Asking for opinions

What did you think of the presentation?
Do you think she's right?
Did you enjoy the dinner?

Asking for information

Would you know what time we break for lunch?
I wonder if you know what time we break for lunch.
Do you happen to know what time we break for lunch?

Get ready

2 Put the conversation in the correct order by placing sentences a–h in sections 1–8 of the Conversation guide on page 23. Two have been done for you.

a Did you? Nice. Do you think that's the best beach in that area?
b I stayed at home.
c Well, we went shopping, but nothing else. It was OK, quite relaxing. What about you?
d I think it probably is, and I don't know why, but it's not so crowded at the weekends.
e Really? Didn't you go out at all?
f We went to the beach at Conil. It was beautiful, we swam for hours.
g What did you do at the weekend?
h Yes, the last time we went to Conil, there was hardly anybody there. It was perfect.

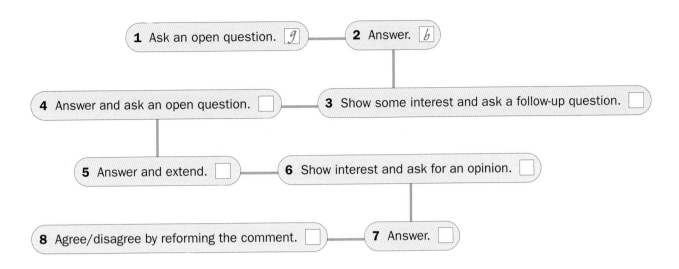

Student A   **Student B**

1 Ask an open question. *g*

2 Answer. *b*

4 Answer and ask an open question. ☐

3 Show some interest and ask a follow-up question. ☐

5 Answer and extend. ☐

6 Show interest and ask for an opinion. ☐

8 Agree/disagree by reforming the comment. ☐

7 Answer. ☐

3 (((10.1))) **Listen and check your answers.**

4 **Practise the conversation with a partner.**

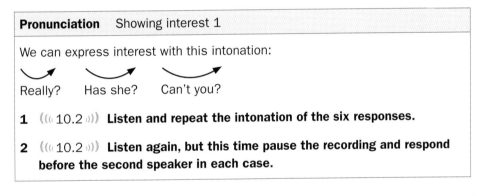

Pronunciation   Showing interest 1

We can express interest with this intonation:

Really?   Has she?   Can't you?

1 (((10.2))) **Listen and repeat the intonation of the six responses.**

2 (((10.2))) **Listen again, but this time pause the recording and respond before the second speaker in each case.**

Task

5 **Work with a partner to make conversations about the topics below. Use the Conversation guide in Exercise 2 as a model.**

last weekend

computers

the last conference you attended

food and drink

music

cars

countries you have visited

sports events

films and books

next weekend

an event in the news

a town you like

11 Difficult calls

Manage difficult phone calls

1 Look at the problems people sometimes have when making a phone call in English (1–5) and match them with the advice (a–f).

1 The conversation is going into topics you don't understand.
2 The other person is speaking too quickly.
3 You start the call, then find you don't know what to say.
4 The other person has just said something using language you don't understand.
5 It's hard to understand because you can't see the other person's lips, facial expressions or gestures.

a Repeat some of the message more slowly and ask the other person to slow down.
b Ask the person to repeat what they said using different words.
c Focus the conversation on the topic you need to discuss.
d Arrange a video call.
e If you're the caller, prepare what you want to say before the call and use notes you have already prepared.

Listening

2 (((11.1))) Listen to a conversation between John Fletcher in London and Hina Sato in Tokyo in which they discuss arrangements for a visit by a senior executive. Decide if these statements are true (T) or false (F).

1 The speakers use modal verbs like *could* and *may* to sound more formal.
2 Hina manages to slow John down.
3 Hina tells John when she doesn't understand something.
4 Hina asks for confirmation of the new arrangements by e-mail.

3 (((11.1))) Read the Key language, then listen again and tick (✓) the ones you hear.

Key language for managing difficult calls

Focus the conversation

I'm calling about …
What I need to know is …

Asking for clarification

So what you're saying is …
Do you mean …?

Show you're listening

Uh-huh. / OK. / Right. / I see

Delaying an answer

I'll need to check and get back to you.
Can I get back to you on that?

Asking for repetition

Sorry, I don't follow you.
Sorry, what do you mean?
Did you say …?
Could you repeat that last part, please?
Could you say/explain that in another way, please?

Asking the other person to slow down

Could you speak a bit more slowly, please?

Asking for confirmation

Could you confirm […] by e-mail, please?

Get ready

4 Use the Key lanaguage to practise the call below with a partner. Read your part first and think about what you can say. When you've finished, swap roles. You may also like to refer to the Key language for telephoning on page 17.

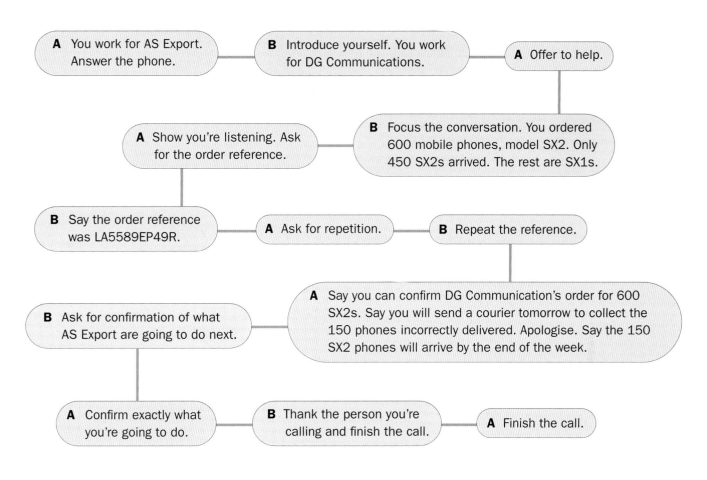

A You work for AS Export. Answer the phone.

B Introduce yourself. You work for DG Communications.

A Offer to help.

B Focus the conversation. You ordered 600 mobile phones, model SX2. Only 450 SX2s arrived. The rest are SX1s.

A Show you're listening. Ask for the order reference.

B Say the order reference was LA5589EP49R.

A Ask for repetition.

B Repeat the reference.

A Say you can confirm DG Communication's order for 600 SX2s. Say you will send a courier tomorrow to collect the 150 phones incorrectly delivered. Apologise. Say the 150 SX2 phones will arrive by the end of the week.

B Ask for confirmation of what AS Export are going to do next.

A Confirm exactly what you're going to do.

B Thank the person you're calling and finish the call.

A Finish the call.

Task

5 Work with a partner. Use the Key language to make the calls below and manage a satisfactory outcome. To prepare to make the calls, you can also check Key language for telephoning on page 17.

Student B: Turn to page 84.

Student A

Make these calls.

1 You're calling your machine-parts supplier because of a quality problem. The last batch of GX parts arrived on time, but you've discovered that their quality isn't up to the standard that you demand. Normally, there's no problem with this supplier, but recently you've placed very large orders with them, and you suspect that they've sub-contracted some of the orders to another manufacturer because they don't have the capacity themselves. This is a breach of your contract with them.

2 You recently travelled from Tokyo to Frankfurt by Easyran Air. You were charged $70 for excess baggage at Tokyo airport because your two suitcases were 7 kilos overweight. You arrived in Frankfurt and waited several hours, but one of your suitcases didn't arrive. It hadn't been put on the flight and arrived three days later. You received some compensation for essential items you had to buy while you were waiting for the case to arrive, but you'd like to have the $70 back because the bag wasn't on your flight.

Receive these calls.

3 You work in a bank. You'll receive a call from a customer with a problem. Deal with the problem, then try to get them interested in one of your new business savings accounts. It offers 1.2% interest.

4 You work for Happy Holidays Travel Agency. You'll receive a call from a dissatisfied customer about a skiing holiday.

12 On time

Talk about time and time management

Listening

1 **Sonja needs to finish a project on time. Read these notes and decide with a partner when she should begin in order to be sure she will meet her deadline.**

- She must finish by 15th May next year.
- She's calculated that the first part of her work will take her three months.
- The second part of her project will take two months, but she can save time by starting this a month before the first part finishes.
- Before she starts the first part, her suppliers should take six weeks to provide her with the materials she needs. However, her suppliers seldom deliver on time. Last time, they were two weeks late.

2 **How important is time in your job? Give two examples.**

3 **You're going to hear a conversation about priorities. A Priority grid is a way of deciding which tasks have to be done straight away and which ones can wait. A marketing manager has the tasks in these notes. Try to arrange them according to their importance and urgency in the Priority grid below.**

'To do' list
1 Assistant Product Manager wants to talk about his idea
2 Call potential customer.
3 Clear back-log of e-mails.
4 Confirm participation in Trade Fair - deadline tomorrow.
5 Draw up a schedule for software training course.
6 Important customer wants call back.
7 Plan next season's marketing campaign.
8 Prepare presentation for next week.
9 Supplier wants to negotiate price.
10 Wash the car.

Priority grid

	Not urgent **Important**	**Urgent** **Important**
importance	Not urgent Unimportant	**Urgent** Unimportant
	urgency	

4 (((12.1))) **Listen to the Marketing Manager talking with her secretary and compare your answer with hers.**

Key language for time

to take
to spend   } time (–ing)
to waste
to save

to meet a deadline
to deliver/finish **by/on** [*day/date*]
in [*month/year*]
within [*period*]
to be **on** time / be late
to be **in** time (for)
to draw up a schedule/timetable

to be delayed
to leave things to the last minute
to prioritise tasks

lead time
urgent tasks
straight/right away

Pronunciation   Diphthongs

1 (((12.2))) **Put these words in the correct column of the table below, according the sound of their diphthongs (in bold). Then listen and check.**

| beer campaign dare dear decide delay gear here know most prepare price |
| priority right share slow so straight their waste |

/aɪ/ **time**	/eɪ/ **main**	/əʊ/ **go**	/eə/ **fair**	/ɪə/ **near**
	campaign			beer

2 Practise saying the words.

Get ready

5 Complete these sentences with the correct form of words from the Key language section.

1 We often .... time doing work which is really not important to the business.
2 The meeting started .... time.
3 I'll do it now, I'll do it .... away.
4 It .... 40 minutes to get to the office from my home.
5 The manufacturing .... time for this product is ten days.
6 This work must be finished .... Friday at the latest.

Task

6 Make notes in your own Priority grid and explain it to your partner. It can include business tasks and things to do out of work.

Follow-up

7 Discuss these questions.
Do you ...

- normally prioritise tasks? How?
- currently have any deadlines to meet? When does the work need to be finished by?
- think you spend most of your time doing the most important tasks in your job?
- often have problems finishing work on time, or have to ask for an extension to a deadline? Why?
- often have to to deal with interruptions to your work?
- spend a lot of your time 'fire-fighting' (dealing with emergencies)?

13 The job interview

Respond
positively
to interview
questions

Put questions
to interviewees

1 What mistakes are these job interviewees making? What should they do?

❶ Sorry, I'm late!

❷ What does your company do?

❸ Why do you want this job?

Because I need a job.

❹ Sorry, do you mind if I take this call?

❺ My last boss was hopeless!

❻ What's the salary?

Any other reasons?

❼ My biggest weakness is that I work too hard.

❽ I don't have any questions at the moment.

Listening

Ms M. Budka

Mr P. Edmondson

2 (((13.1))) **Listen to extracts from two interviews for a job in a bank. Who do you think got the job? Why?**

3 (((13.1))) **Listen again. What were the exact questions asked?**

Key language for an interview

Your strengths	Your experience	Your interests and ambitions
I'm …	In my work, I've …	I'm interested in …
adaptable	worked on	I'm enthusiastic about …
creative	analysed	I'm keen on + *noun*
determined	assisted	I'm keen to + *verb*
efficient	built	In the future, I'd like to …
experienced	carried out	My aim is to …
focused	improved	
hard-working	increased	
loyal	led	
motivated	managed/supervised	
sociable	organised	
practical	planned	
reliable	set up	
	solved	

4 **Which words from *Your strengths* in the Key language section could be used to describe these people? Sometimes more than one adjective is possible.**

1 I find it easy to think of new approaches to work.
2 When I've decided to do a job, nothing can stop me from finishing it.
3 You can trust me.
4 I like to meet clients and socialise with them.
5 I can easily change to suit new situations.
6 Actions interest me more than words.

5 **Which adjectives best describe you?**

6 **Find words in the *Your experience* section which can replace the words in bold. There is sometimes more than one possible answer.**

1 In my last job, I **supported** the sales team.
2 We **developed** new software to process claims.
3 I **headed** a team of engineers.
4 We **did** a reorganisation of the delivery process.
5 We **established** a new export department.
6 I **prepared** a budget for the following year.

7 **How does the form of question A change in question B?**

A Where were you born?
B Can you tell me where you were born?

8 **Use the phrases in column A to transform the direct questions in column B.**

A	B
Could you tell us ...?	Where did you work before your current job?
Tell me ...	When did you leave school?
I'd/We'd like to know ...	Why do you want to work for us?
	What do you know about our company?
	Why did you leave your last job?
	How much do you expect to be paid?

Task

9 **Work with a partner or in two groups: Interview 1 and Interview 2. Think of a job you would like to have. Tell your partner or the other group. Then prepare questions to ask each other.**

Interview 1 questions are on page 86.
Interview 2 questions are on page 85.

10 At the end of the interview, comment on the positive and negative aspects of each others' performances and decide if you got the job.

Follow-up

11 To what extent do you agree with the following?

1 Interviews don't work because they don't test things the candidate will actually need in the job, like technical skills, team work, attitude, etc.
2 Most job interviews are unnatural situations in which the candidate is scared stiff and the interviewer interrogates to find faults rather than positives. Panel interviews make this situation even worse.
3 The interview should be a part of the selection process, but the candidate's references are more important.
4 The only way to really test a candidate is to give him or her a sample of the work to do.

14 My communications

Describe your communication map

Use the language of communication

1 Use the phrases in the box below to say how much you agree with these statements, and why.

"A human being answered the phone!"

> My company communicates with its staff well.

> Communication is good between members of my team.

> I have a good understanding of my company's plans.

> There is too much communication and not enough action where I work.

> Yes, definitely. I tend to agree. I'm not sure.
> I tend to disagree. Definitely not.

Listening

2 (((14.1))) **Akma Hind is the General Manager of RP Consulting, a company in the DF Group, an international employment agency. Listen to her describing her communication map and complete this diagram (1–6).**

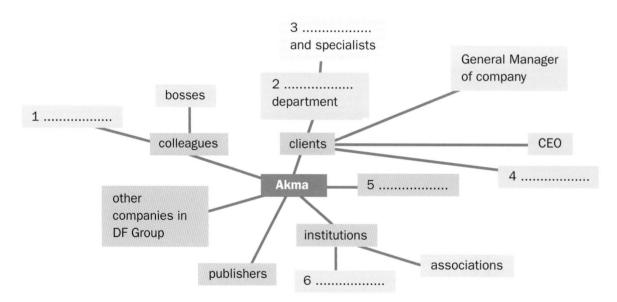

3 (((14.1))) **Listen again and decide if these sentences are true (T) or false (F).**

1 Akma asks her reports to do specific tasks.
2 She discusses proposals and prices with HR Directors.
3 She sometimes talks to the CEOs of clients' companies.
4 Journalists ask her about reward trends.
5 Last month, she spoke to a politician about a research survey.

Key language for communications

Communication verbs + prepositions
I **talked to** Jack **about** the date.
They **asked** us **for** more money.
His boss **shouted at** him when he made a
  mistake.
I **reminded** her **of** the appointment.
They **blamed** me **for** the mistake.
We **warned** them **about** the danger.
He **complained to** the waiter **about** the
  service.
We **had a meeting about** the new
  procedures.
They organised a briefing to **explain** the
  programme **to** us.
He **apologised to** his boss **for** the mistake.
She **commented on** the high quality of the
  goods.
We **argued about** whose fault it was.
She **agreed with** me **about** the solution.
He **insisted on** coming to the meeting.

**Communication verbs
  + direct object + infinitive**
I **told them (not) to** leave.
They **asked him to** pay.
They **advised us not to** go.
We **persuaded/got them to**
  sign the contract.

No preposition
We **discussed** the contract.
They **requested** more time.
I **called/phoned/texted/
  e-mailed** them.

Pronunciation   Weak forms 1

1 (((14.2))) **Listen to the first six sentences in the *Communication verbs
   + prepositions* section of the Key language. How many schwa /ə/ sounds
   can you hear?**

2 (((14.2))) **Listen again and practise saying the sentences.**

Get ready

4 **Work in small groups.**
- Study the verb patterns in the Key language section.
- One member of the group looks at the Key language while the others have
  their books closed.
- That student says one of the verbs; the others must respond as fast as
  possible with the correct preposition. The first person to respond correctly
  must then make a sentence with the verb and preposition to win a point.
- The group member with the most points after five minutes wins.

Task

5 **Draw a communications map for yourself, like Akma's in Exercise 2.**

6 **Discuss these questions about your communications at work.**
- What do you talk about / discuss with each of the people on your map?
- What kind of communication problems do you have in your organisation?
- When was the last time you disagreed with a colleague?
- When was the last time you complained about something?
- Who do you usually e-mail?
- Do you ever argue with people at work? Why? / Why not?
- Which kinds of electronic communication do you prefer? Why?
- What did you discuss in your last meeting?

15 My organisation

Describe your business structure

1 Read about the company Automattic and answer the questions.

1 What do you think are the pros and cons of being a virtual company?
2 Would you like to work in a virtual organisation? Why? / Why not?

AUTOMATTIC

The web development company Automattic is known as a virtual company. Instead of requiring its 123 employees to come into the office every day, everyone works from home. Home may just as easily be Bulgaria, Vietnam or Alabama as San Francisco in the US. It doesn't matter where the employees are, just that they do their job.

Listening

2 (((15.1))) **Yusuf Osman is a human resources executive for KJ Foods Ltd, a food-and-drinks company with its headquarters in Amsterdam, the Netherlands. KJ Foods is a subsidiary of its parent company, Jonson's, in the US. Yusuf describes some different types of organisational structure. Listen and match the types of organisation (1–4) with the organograms (a–d).**

Example: 1 *d*

1 flat   2 business unit   3 functional   4 hierarchical

a
CEO
Marketing | HR | IT | Finance

c
Parent company
Telecommunications | Insurance | Airline

b
CEO
Senior Manager | Senior Manager
Manager | Manager
Assistant | Assistant

d
CEO
Bob | Fred | Kate | Anna

3 (((15.1))) **Listen again and decide if these sentences are true (T) or false (F). Correct any false ones.**

1 Yusuf says organisational structures can be flat or short.
2 Flat organisations have fewer levels of management than hierarchical structures.
3 Functional structures group people together according to product.
4 Business units often contain all the necessary functions like production and marketing.

4 What's the correct hierarchical order of these jobs?

Brand Manager   Assistant Brand Manager
Group Product Manager   Senior Brand Manager
Marketing Director

5 **Sanne Dekker works in the marketing department of KJ Foods. Read what she says about the hierarchy there and check your answer to Exercise 4.**

At the top of the organisation in the Netherlands, there's the President and his staff. We're divided into four business units: cheese, meats, coffee and chocolate. I'm an Assistant Brand Manager in the marketing department of the cheese business unit. I report to the Brand Manager, who's under the Senior Brand Manager, and she reports to the Group Product Manager, who's responsible for four of our brands. Then at the top in our department, there's the Marketing Director.

Pronunciation	Long vowel sounds

1 Find the long vowel sounds in bold that are the same.

> charge   confirm   **ea**rly   hierarchy   law   marketing   parent   reports
> resources   shares   virtual   walk   work   world

2 (((15.2))) **Listen and check.**

3 Practise saying the words.

Key language for business structures

Organisations

The parent company is in …
There are three subsidiaries.
The head office / headquarters in this country is in …
It's divided into departments.
flat vs. hierarchical organisation

Responsibility

Mr/Ms … reports to Mr/Ms …
She's responsible for / in charge of [people, areas]
I'm under the Marketing Manager.

Types of business organisation

A **sole trader** owns his or her own business.
A **partnership** consists of two or more owners of a business, e.g. lawyers.
A **private limited company** (Ltd.) and a **public limited company** (plc) are both owned by shareholders. Anyone can buy plc shares on the stock exchange.
A **non-profit-making organisation** uses its extra funds for the organisation itself.

Get ready

6 **Work with a partner. Use the Key language to ask each other about KJ Foods. If you need help with the answers, check Exercises 2 and 3 on page 32 and Exercise 5 above.**

1 Is KJ Foods a partnership?
2 Is it a subsidiary?
3 Where is the parent company?
4 Where is the headquarters of KJ Foods?
5 What kind of structure does it have?
6 Who's the head of the company?
7 Who's in charge of the marketing department?
8 Who reports to which person in the marketing department?

Task

7 **What kind of an organisation do you work for?**

8 **Draw your company and/or department's organogram.**

9 **Use the Key language to describe your organogram. Who is responsible for what? Who reports to whom?**

16 Our products and services

1 Two of these products or services have generated more than a million dollars in sales. Which?

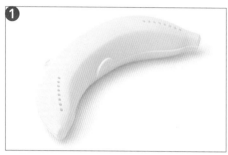

a banana case

a plastic wishbone for vegetarians

a delivery service of cups of tea and coffee

a computer game where players buy and sell virtual farm animals and crops for real cash

2 What's the most useful product or service you've bought this year?

Key language for describing products and services

It's for ...
It's to ...
This means you can / are able to ...
This allows/enables you to ...
This is a new feature.
Compared with / In comparison with ...
The advantage/beauty of this is that ...
We offer ...
With this product/service, you get ...

It's made/composed of ...
It's 60cm long/wide.
It has a length/height/width/depth of ...
They weigh ...
It comes in three sizes/colours.
It has a guarantee/warranty of [period].
The cost price is ...
The retail price is ...

Listening

3 (((16.1))) Listen to four descriptions of products and services. Which is the speaker describing in each pair?

1 marmalade / mayonnaise
2 an investment account / a current account
3 software / a computer
4 a mobile phone / a 3D camcorder

4 (((16.1))) **Listen again and correct *one* word in each of these sentences.**

1 The product needs to be a little creamier for the Spanish market.
2 Interest is paid either monthly or yearly, after tax.
3 You also get free online advice if you have problems.
4 The cost price is very reasonable, just $950.

Pronunciation   Linking 2: /r/

1 (((16.2))) **Listen and notice how the *r* sound at the end of a word is pronounced to link with a vowel sound at the beginning of the next word.**

We take care ͜ of all the problems.
Businesses are ͜ interested in this.
It's for ͜ opening the packaging.

2 (((16.3))) **Listen to and repeat six more examples.**

Get ready

5 **The sentences below (a–l) describe three products or services. Work with a partner and decide:**

1 what the three products or services are
2 which sentences describe which product/service.

a Retired couples are our target market.
b They come in several sizes, with the online retail price of €64.90 for a pair.
c It's password protected.
d Our catalogue includes a wide range of cruises to choose from.
e They only weigh 190g, so they're ideal for long-distance cycle races.
f It's equipped with both USB and micro-USB connections.
g They're extremely strong compared with the competitors' products.
h It allows you to store up to 32,000 songs or 40,000 photos.
i The customer benefits from a full service: travel, hotel bookings, catering and guided tours.
j It's got 130GB of memory, but is only 4cm long.
k They're made of super-strength Kevlar, so they last much longer on tough road surfaces.
l A new feature this year is the 'tailor-made service', which means you can design your own holiday together with our travel consultants.

Task

6 **Describe one of your company's products or services, covering these points.**

Product	Service
purpose	purpose
target market	target market
appearance: size, weight, etc.	customer benefits
packaging	development
cost	quality
price	cost
development	price
features and benefits	possible problems
quality	
range	
possible problems	

17 Processes and procedures

Explain processes and procedures in your work

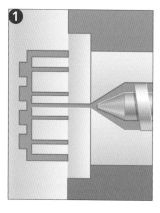
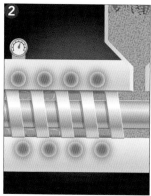

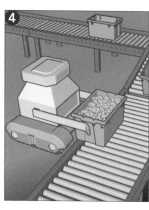

1 Nineteen billion Lego pieces are produced each year. They are made from very tough plastic, the same material used to make hard hats. Match these sentences (a–f) with the pictures showing the production process (1–6).

a After that, the containers are transported by robots to the assembly line. ☐

b Once the plastic has cooled in the moulds, the Lego bits are emptied into containers. ☐

c Then the liquid is forced into moulds. ☐

d Next, the toys are packed on the assembly line. ☐

e Finally, robots prepare the boxes for distribution. ☐

f First of all, the plastic is heated to 230°C. ☐

2 Put sentences a–f from Exercise 1 in the correct order.

Key language for processes and procedures

Present passive structures are often used to describe procedures.
Active: *After an accident, **the insurer investigates the claim**.*
Passive: *After an accident, **the claim is investigated by the insurer**.*

Sequencing
First of all, …
When/Once this has finished, …
After that, …
Then …
Next, …
Finally, …

Pronunciation   Using pauses

1 Where should you pause in these sentences to help to make the message clear?

1 First of all, the plastic is heated to 230°C.
2 Then the liquid is forced into moulds.
3 Once the plastic has cooled in the moulds, the Lego bits are emptied into containers.
4 After that, the containers are transported by robots to the assembly line.
5 Next, the toys are packed on the assembly line.
6 Finally, robots prepare the boxes for distribution.

2 (((•17.1•))) Now listen and check your answers.

3 (((•17.1•))) Listen again and repeat, using the pauses.

Get ready

3 Look at the flow chart. What does it show?

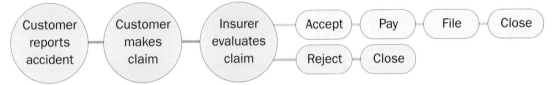

4 Change the words in bold from active to passive.

a If the claim is accepted, **the insurance company pays the customer.**
b **The insurance company evaluates the claim.**
c **The customer makes a claim.**
d **If the insurers reject the claim,** they refuse to pay the customer.
e **The insurers file the paid claim** for future reference.
f **The customer reports the accident** to the insurance company.

5 Put your answers to Exercise 4 in the correct order, using sequencing phrases from the Key language section.

Task

6 Draw a flow chart and describe one or more processes or procedures you are involved with in your job, e.g. software, quality control, production.

18 Socialising 3

Get to know people

1 Do you agree with this advice for people socialising at conferences?

Get there first and leave last.

Dress formally.

Listen more than talk.

Always wear your badge.

Sit with people you don't know.

Only talk to the most important people.

Don't start conversations, wait for people to talk to you.

Listening

2 (((18.1))) Alex Bianchi and Kaito Tanaka are attending a car show. Listen and answer these questions.

1 Who do they work for?
2 What do they have in common?
3 Which country did Alex use to work in?
4 Why is Alex interested in Mercedes?

3 (((18.1))) Listen again and complete these dialogue extracts.

Alex: I work for Fiat, I'm an engineer.
Kaito: Are you? [1]................. . I've just been to the presentation on electric cars.

...

Alex: Oh, I used to work for Ferrari.
Kaito: [2]................. ? Where were you based? In Modena?

...

Kaito: Well, I know Mercedes are recruiting engineers at the moment.
Alex: [3]................. ?

...

Alex: Nice to meet you, Kaito. I'm Alex, Alex Bianchi, and I could really do with a coffee. [4]................. ?

Key language for making good conversation 2

Showing interest/surprise
'I'm one of the speakers.' 'Oh, are you?'
'I used to work for Ferrari.' 'Really, did you?'
'I've met your boss.' 'Have you?'

Asking follow-up questions
How ...?
Why ...?
Where ...? etc.

Agreeing
So [do/have/am/did/was] I.
Neither [do/have/am/did/was] I.

Get ready

4 You can use short questions to express interest or surprise when responding.

A: I live in Rangoon.
B: Really? **Do you?** Were you born there?

(((18.2))) **Listen and respond to the eight statements with *Do you?*, *Has she?*, etc. and a follow-up question as in the example above. Be careful to use the correct auxiliary or modal verb: *do, does, did, have, can*, etc.**

5 To agree, you can use *So* or *Neither*.

A: I sent her an e-mail.
B: So did I.

A: I wasn't at the meeting.
B: Neither was I.

(((18.2))) **Listen again to the sentences in Exercise 4 and respond with surprise and agreement.**

Example: **A:** *I'm leaving tomorrow.*
          B: *Really? Are you? So am I!*

Pronunciation   Showing interest 2

1 (((18.3))) **Listen to the intonation pattern of the response.**

A: I won a prize in the competition.

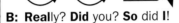

B: Really? Did you? So did I!

2 (((18.4))) **Listen and practise surprised agreement for each statement. Try to reply before the model answer!**

1 I'm lost!
2 I was born on 4th April.
3 Greta's staying at the Five Pines Hotel.
4 She was at the presentation yesterday.
5 I went to Acapulco on holiday last summer.
6 I've got an old Jaguar Mark 2.

Task

6 Work with a partner. Respond with interest/surprise/agreement/ disagreement where appropriate.

Introduce yourselves. Ask about:
- where you're from
- who you work for
- your interests
- your surroundings at the moment
- sport
- traffic
- fashion
- what you'd like to do this evening
- what you think about an event in the news.

Follow-up

7 Discuss these questions.
- Do you think conferences are useful ways of updating your knowledge?
- What's the best conference you've ever attended? Why was it so good?
- Many conferences today have a virtual platform where you participate via a web link. Some people think they don't need to actually attend the conference because of this. Do you agree?

19 Our new product

Talk about preparing and launching your new products and services

A few years ago, two young entrepreneurs were looking for investment in their new business idea, Hungryhouse, a UK-based website for ordering takeaway food online. Users could browse local takeaway menus online using reviews from other customers to help them make their choice. Hungryhouse took a 9% commission on all restaurant orders placed. It also offered a free smartphone app, which allowed users to access the website and order takeaways on the go.

1 Would you invest your money in an idea like this? Why? / Why not?

Listening

2 You're going to hear a talk about the important stages in launching a new product in the mass market. Look at the steps in the Key language section for new products and services. Do you agree with the order of them?

3 (((19.1))) Listen to marketing expert Anita Schlehuber and number the actions she mentions in the Key language section (1–11). There is one action that she doesn't mention.

Key language for new products and services

Clearly define the product.	☐
Come up with ideas.	☐
Develop it.	☐
Do market research.	☐
Evaluate ideas.	☐
Invest in an idea.	☐
Launch the product.	☐
Make some samples.	☐
Promote it in multiple channels.	☐
Test it.	☐
Underline its advantages and benefits.	☐
Calculate the ROI (return on investment).	☐

4 (((19.1))) Listen again and complete the sentences below with the modal verbs in the box.

've got to   have to   mustn't   need to   should   shouldn't

1 First of all, you .... do market research.
2 You .... invest in the idea.
3 You .... try to please everybody with everything.
4 You .... go into full production, of course.
5 I mean you .... make some samples of the product.
6 You .... get your message across.

1 (((19.2))) **Listen to these sentences and answer the questions below.**

We mustn't go into full production yet.
You have to come up with ideas for the new product.

1 Which letter is not pronounced in *mustn't*?
2 How is *have* pronounced in *have to*?

2 (((19.2))) **Listen again and repeat.**

Get ready

5 Look at these comments about various product launches. Use the stages you identified in the Key language section to explain what mistakes were made.

Example: The customers didn't understand why they should buy the product.
The company needed to underline the product's advantages and benefits.

1 The first 10,000 products we made had a design fault.
2 Most of our target customers didn't know the product existed.
3 We didn't realise that the cost of the launch would be so high.
4 It turned out that there was no space in the market for our product.
5 It wasn't clear what our product was!

6 New technology means you could make an electric car which charges in just an hour, compared with other models on the market which require eight hours. Imagine you have invented a car like this. Work with a partner or in groups. Using the Key language as a guide, talk about the steps you would take to launch your car.

Task

7 Make brief notes for a presentation on the way your organisation develops and launches new products or services. Use these questions to help you.

• Has your organisation launched a new product or service in recent years?
• What steps did your company take before the launch?
• When was the launch?
• Who was involved in the launch?
• What were the advantages and benefits of the product/service?
• How did the product/service perform after the launch?
• Is your business currently developing other new products/services?

Follow-up

8 Discuss these questions.

1 Has the manufacturing sector in your country grown or shrunk in recent years? Why?
2 What kind of new products do you think will be popular in the future?
3 Do you think products and services will be more personalised in the future?
4 Will there only be space in the market for large manufacturers in the future?

20 Graphs and charts

Present and describe movements of figures

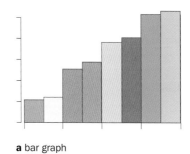

a bar graph

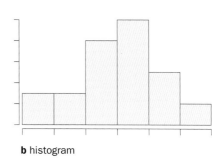

b histogram

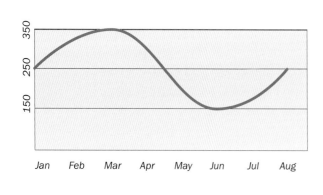

c line graph

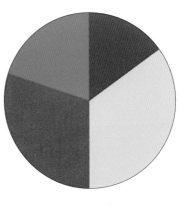

d pie chart

1 Look at the four types of graph above. Which type would you use to show the following?

1 The ice-cream flavours that children prefer
2 The price of gold
3 How much a company's four sales regions contributed to total sales
4 The number of employees in a company related to salary levels

Listening

2 (((20.1))) **Listen to a sales manager comparing the performance of two products across four quarters of the same year, then complete this bar graph.**

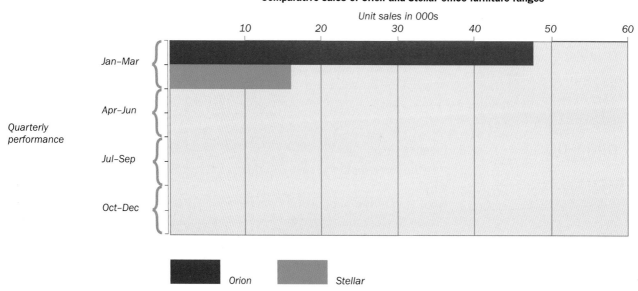

Comparative sales of *Orion* and *Stellar* office furniture ranges

■ Orion   ■ Stellar

Key language for presenting graphs and describing the movement of figures

Introduce the graph
This graph shows/illustrates sales from 2012 to today.
On the horizontal/x axis, ...
On the vertical/y axis, ...

Give an overview
Overall, we can see that sales have improved year on year.
In general, we can see ...

Focusing
Looking at ... in more detail, ...
The most striking feature is ...

Provide details
Sales increased / went up sharply from 100,000 units to 150,000.
Sales rose/grew slightly by 5%.
There was an increase/rise of 25% in sales.

Sales decreased / went down sharply by 50%.
Sales fell/dropped slightly from 100,000 units to 150,000.
There was a fall/drop of 15% in sales.

Sales fluctuated between 20,000 and 90,000.
Sales followed an irregular path.

Sales remained steady/stable.

Sales were 50,000 a month on average.

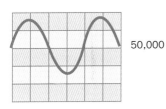

50,000

Sales reached a peak of 150,000.

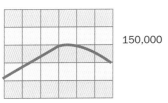

150,000

Pronunciation   Negative prefixes

Negative prefixes like those in the table below are not usually stressed:

Ooo   oOoo
possible   impossible

1   Put these words in the correct column of the table below according to their negative prefix.

~~advantage~~   agree   efficient   formal   legal   likely   logical   lucky   necessary   patient   polite regular   relevant   successful

un-	im-	in-	dis-	il-	ir-
			disadvantage		

2   (((20.2)))   Listen, check your answers and practise saying the words.

Get ready

3   Work with a partner. You're going to describe a graph for your partner to draw. Use the Key language to:

1   introduce your graph
2   give an overview
3   provide details.

Student A: Turn to page 84.
Student B: Turn to page 86.

Task

4   **Present graphs and charts from your business or industry.**

- Introduce your graphs or charts.
- Give overviews.
- Provide details.

Talk about your sales operation

Selling a piano can take a long time, and there are very few repeat purchases. Erica Feidner recently retired after selling more than $41 million of Steinway pianos. Erica matched the customer with a particular piano and preferred the soft sell. Customers said they didn't feel under pressure from her. Instead, they discovered new musical ambitions and a strong desire to own the piano, in spite of the high price.

1 Discuss these questions.

1 What kind of sales or marketing approaches do you respond to best?

2 What kinds of approach do you definitely not respond to?

Listening

2 (((21.1))) **KJC Marinelife make and sell clothing and products for all-weather sailing conditions. Listen to one of the company founders, Henry Clark, talking about their sales channels. Take notes, then describe to a partner the different ways KJC sell their products.**

3 (((21.1))) **Look at the Key language for selling. Listen again and tick (✓) the nine expressions that are mentioned.**

Key language for selling

sales {
discount
force
target
volume
prospect
rep
}

hard/soft sell
to buy in bulk
to negotiate prices
point of sale / retail outlet
indirect sales (*selling to shops and wholesalers*)
direct sales (*selling to the public*)
to invoice a customer
to send an invoice
retail price
salesperson / seller / dealer
goods in stock / out of stock
to sell out of a product
to sell off a product
high visibility
repeat purchases

Pronunciation   Intonation and punctuation

1 (((21.2))) **Listen to and repeat this sentence. Notice the intonation when making lists.**

We sell online, at boat shows, through agents and in our shops.

2 Think about your answers to these questions, then ask a partner, paying attention to the intonation in your answers.

- What products or services does your company sell?
- Where are your customers based?
- Which other countries have you been to?

Get ready

4 Look at these definitions and complete the head word using one word from the Key language section.

1 **sales** .... : a good potential customer for your product
2 .... : a bill for goods or services
3 **sold** .... **of a product**: when you have sold all your stock
4 .... **of sale**: a retail outlet, like a shop
5 .... : a person who buys and sells goods, such as cars
6 **sell** .... **products**: sell goods cheaply
7 **repeat** .... : selling more products to the same customer
8 **sales** .... : the amount of goods sold

Task

5 Prepare to talk about how your organisation sells.

1 Which of the sales channels below does your business use? Why?
2 How do you attract new customers?
3 Do you offer discounts?
4 How big is your sales force?
5 Are repeat purchases common?
6 How do you think your sales could be improved?

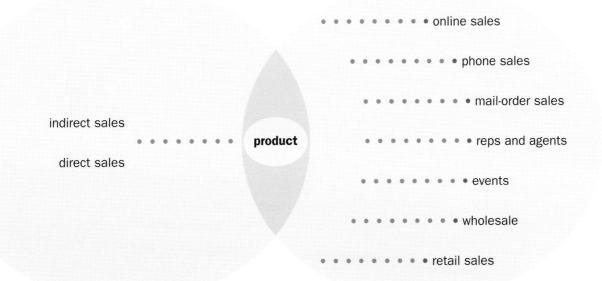

indirect sales

direct sales

product

- online sales
- phone sales
- mail-order sales
- reps and agents
- events
- wholesale
- retail sales

22 Sales performance

Talk about forecasts, targets, performance and results

Listening

1 Which of these opinions do you agree with?

> A good product sells itself.

> Sales targets just cause unnecessary stress.

> If you aim at low sales, you will get low sales.

2 (((22.1))) Min-seo Park launched her Beach Accessories line of products in Asia in 2010. Since then, sales have grown internationally. Which months do you think would be her busiest in South Korea? Listen to a conversation between a sales manager and a seller for Beach Accessories and check your answer.

3 (((22.1))) Listen again and choose the correct options.

1 They've seen *an increase / a decrease* in sales.
2 The sales manager has *achieved / set* a target for the next 12 months.
3 Sales are forecast to *reach / meet* around *$40,000 / $30,000* in the first quarter.
4 He expects sales to *slow down / pick up* in June.
5 Sales will *slow down / remain steady* in the last part of the year.

Key language for sales performance

to set/achieve	a goal / an objective
to make/create	a sales forecast
to set to meet/reach to exceed to miss	} a sales target
Sales	picked up / slowed down / remained steady.
The product performed	badly / quite well overall / well.

Pronunciation Backchaining

Starting at the end of a phrase can help your fluency!

(((22.2))) Listen and repeat the parts of the five sentences you hear.

Example: 1 *in sales – an increase in sales – We've seen an increase in sales.*

Get ready

4 Match these sentences with phrases in the Key language section. In some cases, more than one answer is possible.

❶ You must aim to sell 500 units in the first quarter.

❷ Sales were good for the first six months, but then they were disappointing after June.

❸ They asked me to sell 500, and I sold 800!

❹ We think we'll sell 150,000 units this year.

❺ On the whole, sales were better than we expected.

5 Match the words (1–6) with the descriptions (a–f).

1	performance	a	sales that you want your sellers to aim at
2	forecast	b	an estimate of how well your product will do in the future
3	sales target		
4	product description	c	sales which change according to the time of year
5	like-for-like sales	d	details of the item you're trying to sell
6	seasonal sales	e	how successful your results are
		f	comparing this year's sales to last year's sales under the same conditions

6 Work with a partner. You are both sellers. You each have some information about two products (A and B), their sales targets and forecasts. Talk to each other to complete your table.

Seller A: Turn to page 84.
Seller B: Turn to page 86.

Task

7 Work in small groups. Make brief notes in the table below of a product or service in your business. Choose different products and services where possible. Then meet and describe targets, forecasts and performance.

• Product or service	
• Is it seasonal?	
• Do you focus on new customers, finding new ones or both?	
• How are sales forecasts calculated?	
• Does your sales team usually reach its targets?	
• Are sales targets generally higher than forecasts?	
• What incentives are there for sellers to reach their targets?	
• Have sales increased or decreased over the last two years? Why?	

23 The marketing mix

Talk about marketing your company

1 Think of three of your favourite brands. Briefly tell a partner about them and ask about your partner's favourite brands.

2 Discuss these questions.

1 How did the brands you chose become well known?
2 Which marketing methods do they use?
3 Do you think they outsell the competition? How?

Listening

3 (((23.1))) **Marketing experts sometimes group areas for success into 'the five Ps' (as shown in the diagram on page 49). Listen to marketing analyst Ben Richards discussing the marketing mix of Manchester United Football Club and complete these notes.**

1 Products include .... such as the sale of shirts and a range of memorabilia, books and programmes.
2 Manchester United books, shirts, programmes and many other items are sold and .... through its website.
3 The product also relates to ....
4 Manchester United is a global ....
5 The club has a range of joint ....
6 The club has positioned itself at the premier end of the market and charges ....

4 (((23.1))) **Listen again and find examples of the five Ps using the Key language on page 49 to help you.**

Get ready

5 Look at the five Ps of marketing in the Key language section and match the sentence halves.

1 Product is the 'thing'
2 Price is what it
3 Place is when and
4 Promotion is communication with your
5 People is the human

a contact between your customer and your business.
b customers which leads to brand recognition.
c that influences customer perception.
d where your product is available to customers.
e costs the customer to use your product.

6 Work with a partner or in small groups. Use the Key language to discuss the possible marketing mix of these businesses.

• A company that makes video-game consoles
• A travel agency specialising in holidays for pensioners
• A company that makes high-quality skincare products

Key language of the marketing mix

Product

We offer
{ a high-end
an easy-to-use
a low-cost
an easily available }
product/service.

Our merchandising includes branded-goods sales.
We are positioned at the high/low end / mid-point
of the market.

Place

We sell direct to the customer.
You can order this through catalogues /
by mail order / online.
We are active at trade shows.
You can find us in stores throughout (Asia).

Price

This is a high-cost, high-quality product/service.
It's cheaper than other products on the market.
It's a heavily discounted item.

Promotion

If you buy a large quantity, we can offer a 10% discount.
We offer competitive terms and conditions.

People

We select/recruit/hire people with the best skills and
abilities to do the job.
We provide our staff with appropriate training.
We offer excellent after-sales support.

PLACE
Retail
Wholesale
Mail order
Internet
Direct sales

PRICE
Profit margins
List price
Discounts
Loss leader

TARGET MARKET

PROMOTION
Special offers
Leaflets/Posters
Direct mailing
Advertising
Free gifts
Competitions

PRODUCT
Design
Technology
Convenience
Merchandising
Value
Packaging
Branding
Accessories
Warranties
Quality

PEOPLE
Employees
Management
Culture
Customer
service

Task

7   You're going to present the marketing mix of your company. Use the Key
language and audio script 23.1 on page 92 to help you prepare, then
present your ideas to the class.

24 Social networking

Talk about using social networking in your business

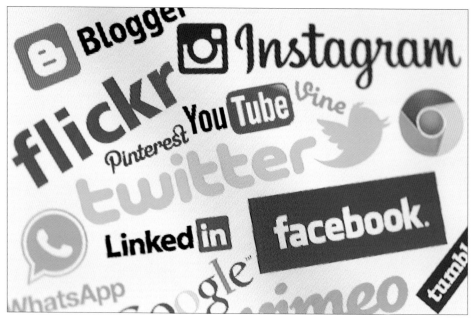

1 Discuss these questions.

1 Do you use any of the social networking sites shown above?

2 Are you on Facebook? Which of these answers is closest to your opinion?

> Yes, of course. I couldn't live without it.

> I am, but I don't use it all the time.

> Definitely not. If I want to talk to someone, I'll meet them or give them a ring.

3 If you use social networking sites, what do you use them for? If you don't, why not?

Listening

2 Vicky is Communications and Marketing Manager at Fresh Egg, an internet marketing agency. You're going to hear her talk about how she uses social networking in her job. Tick (✓) the Key language you think she might use.

Key language for talking about social networking in business

Communicating actions
to post a message / an event / an activity
to keep in touch (via Twitter/Facebook) with
to write/keep a (live) blog

How does it help?
information at your fingertips
immediate feedback
to improve customer communication / realtime communication
networking tool

What can you do?
to get news and information out
to interact digitally
to engage with clients
to expand contact base
to keep up to date with
to do market research

3 (((24.1))) **Listen and see if you were correct.**

4 (((24.1))) **Listen again and correct these statements.**

1 Five years ago, we used to send letters and catalogues out to customers.
2 Customer communication has not improved a lot.
3 We can get immediate feedback if suppliers are happy with something and if they have any problems.
4 Analysis is also an important part of my job.
5 Through social networking, I can keep in touch with my clients.

Pronunciation *used to*

The *d* in the modal verb *used to* is not pronounced.

1 (((24.2))) **Listen to and repeat these sentences.**

We used to send letters and leaflets.
We used to produce paper catalogues.
Requesting confirmation used to be very slow.

2 Think of three things you used to do when you were younger. Tell your partner.

Get ready

5 Match the sentence halves.

1 We used to send hundreds of letters to clients by post, but now it is much easier
2 We used to produce paper catalogues twice a year, but now customers have all
3 All our market research was done by phone or face to face, but now we ask for
4 Meetings with foreign clients were expensive and time-consuming, but now we can
5 Finding and contacting potential clients was mainly through cold-calling,

a but now we use sites like Foursquare as a fast and efficient networking tool.
b customer feedback on our products via Twitter.
c the information at their fingertips. They can see our latest products and collections online.
d interact digitally face to face, which saves time and money.
e and quicker to engage with them online, and all correspondence is digital.

Task

6 French IT company Atos is planning to ban internal e-mail and use an internal social network instead. CEO Tierry Breton says this will make them more efficient and save time. (Currently employees spend 15 to 20 hours a week checking and answering internal e-mails.)

Discuss social networking and communication in your organisation by answering these questions.

1 Some people believe that social networking sites can be a dangerous tool and should be banned in companies. What reasons can you think of for this? Do you agree or disagree?
2 Do you think that the strategy of Atos would work in your company? Why? / Why not?
3 What changes has your company made to the way it communicates, both internally and with customers, in the past five years?
4 What other changes could be made to your company to improve communication? Work with a partner to create a list of guidelines to improve communication policy in your organisation.

Give opinions, agree and disagree

1 React to these statements with opinions from the box below. Give reasons for your choices.

1 Meetings organised to provide information are pointless. We can all read.
2 There's no point in having a meeting if it's not followed by an action plan.
3 Keeping to a strict timetable in meetings makes it impossible to come to the best decisions.
4 The chairperson should encourage disagreement – there's no point in a meeting where everyone agrees.
5 If a participant is late, they shouldn't be invited to the next meeting.
6 Don't send participants a copy of the agenda before the meeting or they'll make their minds up before the meeting starts.

> That's right. I agree on the whole. It depends on …
> I disagree on the whole. I don't agree.

Key language for participating in discussions

Checking understanding
So what you're suggesting is …
So in other words, what you're saying is … Is that right?
Does that mean …?
Are you saying …?

Giving opinions and suggestions
(*in approximate order of strength*)
I definitely think we should …
There's no point in (–ing)
In my opinion/view, …
I think / don't think …
It seems to me …
Why don't we …?
It might be an idea to …
How about (–ing)?

Agreeing and disagreeing

Agree
Yes, I agree entirely.
I agree. / That's right.
I think Tom's right.
Yes, good idea!

Agree in part
I agree on the whole, but …
I agree up to a point; however, …
I see what you mean, although …

Disagree and propose alternative
No, I don't agree because … It'd be better to …
I can't agree with that. Wouldn't it be better to …?
I disagree entirely.

Interrupting
Could I just say something here / make a point about that?
Sorry to interrupt, but …
Could I just come in here?

Returning to a point
As I was saying, …
Coming back to what I was saying, …
Could we go back to …?

Listening

2 You're going to hear an extract from a meeting at which this problem was raised. How would you deal with it?

The Senior Accountant, Carmel Robinson, has reported that accounts show one of your main customers, Hobsons, owed your company $280,000 at the end of last month. This month, the same account shows a debt of $270,000, although apparently no payments have been made. She can find no explanation for this.

3 (((25.1))) Listen to the extract of the meeting. Which two possible explanations are given for the missing money?

4 (((25.1))) **Listen again and complete these transcript extracts with phrases from the Key language section.**

Mark: And Hobsons made no payment in April, you're sure of that?

Carmel: Absolutely.

Naresh: [1]................. that somebody here has been falsifying the accounts?

...

Mark: We have to find out what happened here first.

Carmel: [2]................. . There's no point in bringing them into it at this stage. First of all, we have to carry out an audit here.

Naresh: Yes, [3]................. , but it might be an idea to invite somebody from outside to do the audit.

...

Mark: First of all, we'll do an internal check, and if that doesn't turn up anything, we'll take it to the next stage.

Su: [4]................. ? This isn't the first time this has happened, you know ...

Pronunciation Weak forms 2

In fast spoken English, these words are often pronounced using the /ə/ sound: *to, for, from, a, as, of, that* (conj.), *about, are*.

1 (((25.2))) **Listen and complete these sentences with words containing the /ə/ sound.**

1 I'd like .... welcome Mr Kaya .... Turkey.
2 It seems to me .... there are two problems.
3 It's very important .... you have .... clear idea .... this.
4 It's .... fast .... lightning.
5 There .... three reasons .... this.
6 Could I just make .... point about that?
7 How .... trying another supplier?

2 (((25.2))) **Listen again and repeat.**

Task

5 **You are members of a staff committee. You're having a meeting to discuss the issues below. Order them according to priority, then use the Key language to exchange opinions and decide what to do.**

a It's been suggested that every year, the company should reward a member of staff for work done. Is this a good idea? If so, what kind of reward should be given?

b One of the factory workers has been slightly injured by the machinery he was working with on the assembly line. He's threatening to sue the company. This is the third time he's been injured this year. On the other two occasions, he had a week off work due to minor injuries. On those occasions, no compensation was paid.

c The coffee machine is broken again, the water cooler doesn't cool the water and the snack machine often takes money without dispensing anything. The same company supplies all three machines and maintains them. Other suppliers cost 20% more.

d Your IT consultants need to visit their clients, so they have a company car as part of their salary package. However, some consultants do most of their work from the office, and management are thinking of terminating the car leasing agreement for these employees when they expire next month.

26 Socialising 4

Develop fluency

Task	**Play *Talk about* ... with a partner or in small groups.**
	• Each player chooses a counter and places it on the START square.
	• Toss a coin: if it's 'heads', move your counter one square; if it's 'tails', move two squares.
	• Talk for a minute about the topic on the square you land on. If you hesitate for too long, move one square backward; if you manage to speak for a minute, move two squares forward.
	• Allow a maximum of ten seconds' thinking time before each player speaks.

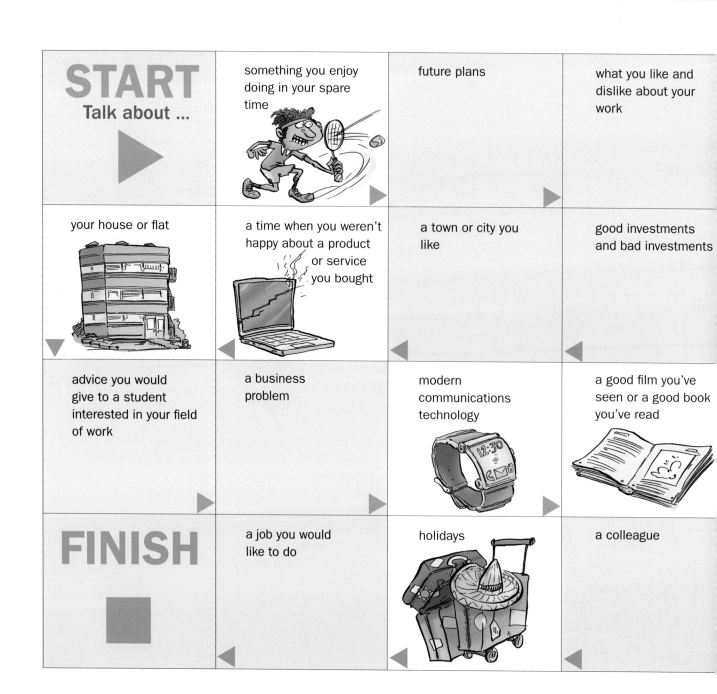

START Talk about ... ▶	something you enjoy doing in your spare time ▶	future plans ▶	what you like and dislike about your work ▶
your house or flat ◀	a time when you weren't happy about a product or service you bought ◀	a town or city you like ◀	good investments and bad investments ◀
advice you would give to a student interested in your field of work ▶	a business problem ▶	modern communications technology ▶	a good film you've seen or a good book you've read ▶
FINISH ■ ◀	a job you would like to do ◀	holidays ◀	a colleague ◀

Key language for fillers

We use fillers when we want time to think. They can be useful to avoid hesitation, but be careful not to use them too much.

right	I mean
well	sort of
so	uh /ʌ/
actually	er /ɜː/
basically	um /ʌm/

a trip you made	a country you have visited	something you would like to have	your industry
the news	what makes a good leader	how you spent last weekend	food
what makes a company successful	interesting websites	your journey to work	customers
advertising	shopping	your responsibilities at work	the environment

27 SWOT analysis

Evaluate aspects of your business using SWOT

SWOT analysis is a tool to help people understand and make decisions. It stands for Strengths, Weaknesses, Opportunities and Threats and can be used to analyse an industry, a company, a business unit, a project, an idea or even a choice of career.

Listening

1 You're going to hear a conversation between James and his business partner, Emma. They own a café in Sydney and have been taking a look at their business. Put these sentences in the correct section of the chart below.

1 A new large office development is being built opposite.
2 There is only space for four tables in the café.
3 Next month, a new restaurant is opening 100 metres away.
4 The café is in the centre of the city.

Strengths	Weaknesses
Opportunities	**Threats**

2 (((27.1))) **Listen to the conversation and complete the chart in Exercise 1.**

Key language for suggesting advice

If I were you, I'd ...
You should ...
Why don't you ...?
You could/might ...
Couldn't you ...?
It might be an idea to ...
I suppose you could ...

↑ sure
↓ less sure

Get ready

3 Use the Key language to suggest advice to James and Emma for dealing with these weaknesses and threats.

1 There's only space for four tables in the café.
2 They haven't got an alcohol licence.
3 The kitchen is very small.
4 Next month, a new restaurant is opening 100 metres away.
5 The owner of their building is likely to put the rent up soon.

Pronunciation   Weak forms 3

Grammatical words like auxiliary verbs, prepositions, conjunctions and modal verbs are usually unstressed

1 Mark the unstressed words in these sentences.

1 What was the name of the restaurant?
2 If I were you, I'd look for a new office.
3 We're going to look at the strengths, weaknesses, opportunities and threats.
4 Some customers can sit outside.
5 We should definitely think about starting a website so customers could order food and drinks at their desks.

2 (((27.2))) **Listen, check your answers and practise saying the sentences.**

Task

4 Make notes in the chart for your own business/industry/project, etc. and prepare to talk about it.

Strengths	Weaknesses
Opportunities	Threats

Follow-up

5 Make suggestions about each other's analyses.

Example: *You face a threat from your competitors. Why don't you reduce your prices?*

28 Appraisals

Talk about appraisal processes in companies

1 Discuss these questions.

1 Does your company review employee performances regularly?

2 Which of these answers best reflects your situation?

> No. I've never had an appraisal.

> Yes, they hold appraisals every year.

> Yes, we have regular appraisals throughout the year.

2 Look at these reasons for companies to give their employees performance appraisals. Which do you think are the most important?

a to improve the company's productivity

b to make decisions regarding promotion, job changes and termination

c to review salaries

d to identify what is required to perform a job (goals and responsibilities of the job)

e to assess an employee's performance against company goals

f to help employees improve their performance

g to allow an employee to give their opinion/feedback on the company

h to identify staff training requirements

Listening

3 (((28.1–28.3))) What is the purpose of these three appraisals? Listen and match each appraisal (1–3) with one of the reasons in Exercise 2 (a–h).

4 Look at the audio scripts on page 93 and underline phrases that mean the following.

1 You want something else. / The suggestion/offer is not good enough.

2 You have a proposal. / Making an offer

3 Giving an opinion / a suggestion

4 Summarising what has been said before

5 Agreeing

6 Giving bad news

Pronunciation Silent letters

1 Cross out the silent letters in these words.

answering	guest	sign
biscuit	guide	vehicle
business	high	Wednesday
calm	hour	whole
debt	island	would

2 (((28.4))) Listen and check your answers.

58

Key language for appraisals

Main duties and responsibilities

This year / Recently, I've { been working on the ABC project.
been managing European accounts.
been dealing with Malaysian customers.

Areas of ability and qualities

time management	creativity
communication skills	problem-solving and decision-making
administrative skills	teamwork
IT/equipment/machinery skills	leadership qualities
product/technical knowledge	ability to work under pressure

Interviewer

Let's look at your current performance / past performance.
We've been really impressed with …
Your (teamwork) is of a high level.
However, there is room for improvement.
We're concerned about …
career goals: short/medium/long term
areas to improve

Let's agree { an action plan for next year.
on specific objectives.

Employee

I believe that I've performed well.
I achieved my objectives (for the year).
Under the circumstances, I think I've done well.

I agree that there's room for improvement, but …
I know there have been problems, but …
I'd like to explain why this has happened.

I'd like to discuss my salary / possibilities of promotion.

I feel I need (more training).

Get ready

5 **Which of these questions are asked by the interviewer in an appraisal interview (I), and which are asked by the employee (E)?**

1 What have been your key achievements and successes?
2 Are there any skills or areas of your job that you would like to develop?
3 What do you like/dislike about working for this company?
4 What did I do well this year?
5 What gives you the most satisfaction in your work?
6 What areas do I need to develop?
7 What are the most difficult areas in your job?
8 How do you see your career developing in the next five years?
9 Is there a possibility of promotion?
10 Will there be a pay increase this year?
11 What are your goals for me between now and our next review?
12 What can I do to improve the company?

Task

6 **Work with a partner. Hold appraisal interviews with each other, taking it in turns to be the interviewer and the employee. Remember to look at general abilities as well as performance and goals.**

29 Profit and loss

Use the language of profit and loss

Jim Christy, the founder of Incredible Foods, a dessert-delivery service in Pennsylvania, thought he'd hit the big time when his business expanded rapidly and got one of the biggest accounts of all: Starbucks. But although revenues reached $3.4 million in 2005, the cost of fuel, employee benefits and insurance made the business unprofitable. That year, he decided to downsize and focused his marketing attention on local customers. The following year, he saw an 11% increase in profits on revenues of $2.2 million.

1 What does Jim Christy's story tell us about profits?

2 It's possible for a company to make a profit on paper and yet still go bankrupt. How do you think this could happen?

Key language for profit-and-loss entries

The **profit-and-loss account** (or **P&L** or **income statement**) balances income against expenses to determine the profit or loss over a period of time – often six months or a year. In most countries, the law requires companies to produce an annual profit-and-loss account.

The top part of the P&L account shows the **income from sales**, or the **turnover**. The deduction of the **direct costs** or **cost of sales** produces the **gross profit**.

The second part of the P&L shows the **indirect costs**, or **overheads**, such as heating and lighting. After deducting these, you have the **operating profit**. Once tax and interest charges are deducted, you arrive at the bottom line: the **net profit**.

Other income terms
revenue (AmE) / turnover (BrE): total sales
EBIT: earnings before interest and taxes
operating profit: gross profit after operating expenses
ROI: return on investment

Pronunciation   Linking 3: /w/

When a word ends with the sounds /əʊ/ or /uː/ and the next word begins with a vowel sound, they're often linked with /w/.

Our company has a high turnover, so⌣of course we need to prepare P&L accounts often.
We send the accounts to⌣our shareholders.
We talk to⌣each other every week about revenues.

1 Mark where the linking sound /w/ occurs in these sentences.

1 These figures show earnings for the first six months.
2 Do I have to sign here?
3 Go to our homepage to find the link to the accounts.
4 I wanted to ask you about the overheads.
5 See you again soon.

2 (((29.1))) Listen and repeat.

3 Complete the definitions with words from the Key language section.

1 .... , or turnover, is at the top of the P&L.
2 Labour and materials are .... costs.
3 The .... profit is calculated after direct costs have been deducted.
4 After the gross profit, the next line of profit before tax and interest is the
  ....
5 Rent and the internet are examples of .... costs.
6 The bottom line is the .... , which shows earnings after
  tax and interest have been paid.
7 The .... is the ratio of money gained or lost on an investment in
  relation to the amount of money invested.

4 (((29.2))) Listen and check your answers.

Task

**5 Work with a partner. Look at the balance sheet below and calculate the
profit lines for 22nd Century Games plc for 2013 and 2014.**

6 What would you do if this was your company? Why?

22ND CENTURY GAMES PLC

Profit-and-loss account	2013	2014
Turnover	500,000	500,000
Less cost of sales:		
Labour	100,000	100,000
Materials	100,000	130,000
Gross profit	1.............	4.............
Less indirect costs:		
Salaries	120,000	140,000
Consultancy fees	6,000	20,000
Admin	16,000	17,000
Rent	15,000	35,000
Electricity	4,000	5,000
Telephone, internet	2,000	3,000
Fuel	5,000	18,000
Insurance	2,000	2,000
Operating profit	2.............	5.............
Less tax	30,000	27,000
Net profit/loss	3.............	6.............

Follow-up

**7 Present and explain annual P&L results from your company or those of a
competitor.**

30 Meetings 2

Lead and structure meetings

1 **Match these types of people who attend meetings (1–8) with the descriptions (a–h)**

They …

1 the Builder	a	tend to agree with nearly everything.
2 the Expert	b	don't participate until making a comment at the end of the meeting.
3 the Interrupter	c	often go off the point.
4 the Silent One	d	are good at focusing the group on the important issues.
5 the Supporter	e	think they must talk as much as possible.
6 the Talker	f	are constructive, productive and reasonable.
7 the Guide	g	constantly interrupt others while they are speaking.
8 the Wanderer	h	think they know everything about the topic.

2 **Discuss these questions.**

1 Which of the types are positive?
2 Do you know anybody who fits these descriptions? Which type are you?
3 What can the chairperson of a meeting do to manage some of these people?

Listening

3 (((30.1))) **You're going to hear a chairperson manage parts of a staff meeting at a car manufacturer. Listen and decide if these statements are true (T) or false (F). Correct the false ones.**

1 The chairperson wants to finish by five o'clock.
2 The most urgent problem is that of the steering-wheel lock.
3 William interrupts the chairperson.
4 Jasmine is a 'Supporter' type.
5 There has been only one complaint from Western Garages.
6 The PX3 model has a warranty of four years.
7 Simona is going to check the company's legal position concerning the PX3 model.

4 (((30.1))) **Look at the Key language on page 63. Then listen again and tick (✓) the phrases you hear.**

Key language for chairing meetings

Starting the meeting
Good afternoon, everybody.
OK, shall we start?
Does everyone have a copy of the agenda?

Explaining the purpose of the meeting
The reason we're here today is to …
discuss / consider / decide on a number of issues

Timing
I'd like to aim for a (three o'clock) finish.

Prioritising and starting
The most urgent matter is …
We're going to start with …
The first/main point on the agenda is …
Perhaps we could start by looking at …

Asking for opinions
Can we go round the table on this?
What do you think about this, (Luca)?
What are your views on this, (Jon)?
Do you agree, (Petra)?
Has anyone got anything to add?

Moving the meeting on
Let's move/go on to the next point on the agenda.
Moving on to the next matter …
Now we come to …

Reacting to interruptions
I suggest we deal with that point later / at next
    week's meeting.

Actioning
(Cathy), I want you to …
(Takumi), you're going to …
(Kurt), it's your job to …

Closing the meeting
So, to summarise the main points, …
Right, that's all for today.
I think we should call it a day there.
Let's meet again on 3rd December to follow up on /
    confirm / check progress / clear up any issues /
    report back on …

Task

5 **Work in groups or with a partner. You are a committee which represents the company staff. You're going to meet to discuss the issues below. Order the agenda 1–5 according to priority.**

a   The level of ignorance about software in the company has never been higher. Certain jobs take much longer than they should because some people don't know how to use programs like Excel properly. The budget allocation for training is very low this year.

b   Last year, the company made a slight loss. Senior management have just awarded themselves a 10% salary increase, with the Managing Director getting 20%. Employees below these levels, including yourselves, have not received a rise in five years.

c   Your company is applying for environmental certification. In preparation, it's been decided to hold a training day on the importance of responsible environmental actions which the company and staff can take. You need to come up with some general ideas to promote on the training day.

d   It will soon be time again for the end-of-year party. Last year, this was held in the office, but there were problems. There was damage to property of over €1,000, a lot of people who came hadn't been invited, and at one o'clock in the morning, the police arrived after complaints from people living in the neighbourhood.

e   You've been asked to suggest a hotel in your town to host a conference in three months' time. What factors do you need to take into consideration when choosing a hotel? Who's going to be responsible for making arrangements with the hotel you choose?

6 **Study the Key language in this unit and on page 52. Decide on a chairperson and begin your meeting.**

7 **Plan an agenda of issues o discuss concerning your own workplace(s) and hold a meeting.**

31 Recruitment

Talk about recruitment processes

1 When hiring new staff, some companies use an external recruitment agency, and some companies use their own human resources department. Which of the phrases below support each method? Write RA (recruitment agency) or HR (human resources) next to them.

1 knowledge of internal candidates ......
2 extensive candidate database ......
3 understands the company's needs ......
4 dedicated recruitment experience ......
5 wider range of advertising options ......
6 no agency fee ......

2 Discuss the advantages and disadvantages of both options mentioned in Exercise 1.

Listening

3 (((31.1))) Listen to part of an interview with Amir Aman, a human resources manager with AON Hewitt, a management consultancy firm. He's talking about the recruitment process used at his company. Then answer these questions.

1 What does Amir do?
2 How does he advertise job openings?
3 Why do they look at CVs?
4 How many references are required?
5 Who is present at the final interview?
6 What two things are included in the terms of contract?

4 (((31.1))) Listen to the interview again and complete these steps in the recruitment process.

1 ....
2 Look at CVs, group applicants and create a shortlist.
3 ....
4 Ask for referees and get letters of reference.
5 ....
6 Conduct third interview with at least two department managers.
7 ....
8 Take candidate on.

Pronunciation Making statements into questions with rising intonation

It's possible to change statements into *yes/no* questions by using a rising intonation.

⟶

And then you hire them?

1 (((31.2))) Listen to and repeat these questions.

You like working in teams?
He's finished already?
Your CV is up to date?
You're leaving now?
This is the last interview?

2 Prepare three similar questions to ask others in the class about their lives, jobs, etc.

Key language for recruitment

First step
to advertise a job opening / a vacancy
to apply to a company for (a job / a position)
to complete an application form

Screening

Candidates need to provide { a covering e-mail/letter.
an updated copy of their CV/resumé.
a recent photograph.

shortlist of applicants / to be shortlisted (for a job)
to review applicants
to schedule interviews

The interview/selection process
to have a(n) telephone/online/first/second/final interview
to pass/fail the selection process
to ask for referees / references / a letter of reference
to check references

Selection
to make the candidate an offer
to negotiate the job offer/terms
start date / salary and benefits / probationary period / holiday entitlement

Join a company
to recruit / hire / take on
to employ full-time / part-time / on a short-term contract / on a permanent contract

---

Get ready

5 Work with a partner and discuss:

- what sort of recruitment process is required to hire someone for the jobs shown below
- the sort of skills required for each job, and why.

 shop assistant

telesales operator

sales executive

Task

6 In groups, consider the recruitment policy in your company and compare it to the one that Amir Aman described in Exercise 3. You may like to think about these questions.

- How are staff recruited in your company?
- Do you use a recruitment agency or your own HR department?
- What was the process you experienced when you were hired?
- What do you remember most about the experience?
- Is there anything you would change about the process?

Follow-up

7 In the interview, Amir mentions company benefits such as private pension, healthcare, car, etc. What other benefits can you think of that companies offer?

8 Which benefits do you think are most important? Why?

Make predictions

cleantech

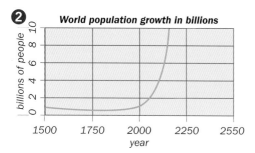

World population growth in billions

major emerging national economies → BRICS (Brazil, Russia, India, China, South Africa)

internet sales

1 **Describe possible trends and make predictions suggested by the images above.**

Example: 1 *The cleantech sector is expanding and will continue to grow globally in the 21st century.*

2 **Do you see these as opportunities or threats?**

Key language for making predictions

* *will* and *going to* are both used for predicting future events.
  *I think Brazil, Russia, India, China and South Africa **will continue** to be the main engines of the world's economic growth.*
  *On current trends, we**'re going to** see more of this in the future.*

* *might* is used to express doubt about predictions.
  *This **might** become very controversial.*

* *likely* and *unlikely* are used to talk about the probability of events.
  *Companies in the future are **likely** to want more and more data about customers.*
  (= Companies in the future will probably want more and more data about customers.)
  *She's **unlikely** to come to the meeting.*
  (= She probably won't come to the meeting.)

* *bound to* is used to express certainty that something will happen.
  *The population is **bound to** grow.*
  (= The population will certainly grow.)

Listening

3 (((32.1))) **Listen to an economist describing how she sees the future of business. Which of the trends in the images above does she discuss?**

4 (((32.1))) **Listen again. Which of the following does she say?**

1 Customers will want more information about companies.
2 International industries and governments will co-operate more.
3 The digital revolution will carry on.
4 In some countries, there are more people leaving employment than entering it.
5 India's young workforce might be an enormous asset to their economy in the future.
6 The BRICS countries will continue to drive growth in the world economy.

Get ready

5 Choose the best verbs to complete the sentences.

1 I've invited Chun to the meeting, but I don't think she *'ll / might* be able to come.
2 They're too expensive. They *aren't going to / might not* sell many at that price.
3 They always ask for a discount, so they're *bound / unlikely* to ask for a discount this time as well.
4 I haven't decided about the conference yet. I *won't / might not* go.
5 Their party is quite unpopular at the moment, so they're *likely / bound* to lose the next election.
6 I don't know when they'll call – I suppose they *'re going to / might* call this afternoon.
7 The score is 3–0 to Bayern with five minutes to go, so it looks like they *'re going to / might* win the cup.
8 I'm not sure what type of car I want. I *'ll / might* buy a Honda.

Pronunciation *will* and *won't*

1 (((32.2))) **Be careful not to confuse the pronunciation of *won't* and *want*. Listen and circle the sentences you hear.**

1	I won't go.	I want to go.
2	They won't come.	They want to come.
3	You won't do it.	You want to do it.
4	We won't pay the bill.	We want to pay the bill.

2 (((32.3))) **Listen and repeat the pairs of sentences.**

3 (((32.4))) **Listen and circle the sentences you hear.**

1	I go.	I'll go.
2	We help you.	We'll help you.
3	You work hard.	You'll work hard.
4	They play golf.	They'll play golf.

4 (((32.5))) **Listen and repeat the pairs of sentences.**

Task

6 Make notes on predictions about the categories in this table, then talk about them using the Key language.

My industry	My company	My department	Me

33 Contingency planning

Discuss your plans in case of future events

1 Contingency planning is about asking and answering *What if ...?* questions. What would you do in these situations?

1 Your computer breaks down with message: *Virus attack – total data loss.*
2 A competitor has made damaging accusations about your company on social media.
3 The fire bell in your office rings.
4 Your main supplier goes bankrupt. Without them, you can't do business.
5 You make a mistake that's likely to cost your company a lot of money. Only you know about it.
6 You receive an offer of a much better job abroad. Your partner doesn't want to go.

Listening

2 (((33.1))) **Phil and Kate Entwistle run a medium-sized hotel in Cornwall, England. They've decided they need to prepare some contingency plans. Listen and answer these questions.**

1 What are the key areas of their business?
2 Make a list of the kinds of risk they identify.
3 What would they do if there were a flood?

Key language for discussing contingencies

Describing probability
... is a real risk.
... might/may/could happen.
... is a slight possibility.

Discussing possible events
What would you do if ... happened?
If ... happened, I'd ...

Being proactive instead of waiting for things to happen
I/We should ... in case (the town floods).
I/We should ... in case of (flooding).
I/We should / ought to ... now.

Get ready

3 Match the sentence halves.

1 If the value of the dollar continues to increase,
2 We should try to get guarantees from the bank
3 We ought to insure
4 Who would take charge of the department
5 Flooding in this area
6 We should open a special credit account in case
7 If there was another transport strike,
8 What would you

a against fire and theft.
b if your sales manager left the company?
c in case we have cashflow problems.
d is a real risk.
e of bad debts.
f we might have to find suppliers in another country.
g do if the price of gold suddenly dropped?
h we'd have big problems with deliveries.

Pronunciation   Conditionals and contractions

In spoken conditional sentences, contractions are normally used.

1 Rewrite these sentences using contractions.

1 If there was a flood, we would need to evacuate the hotel.
2 If a customer did not pay, I would speak to them first.
3 If we are late, we will have to take a taxi.
4 If you call me tomorrow, I will tell you the details.

2 Practise saying the sentences with the contractions.

Task

4 Make brief notes in the table below on some of the risks that may affect your job or business, and the contingency plans you could adopt. (See examples below.)

5 Discuss your risks and plans with a partner.

Risks	Contingency plan
financial *non-payment by a customer*	*If a customer didn't pay, I'd speak to them first.*
technical *loss of data*	*I should back up my computer system in case of a loss of data.*
operational	
reputational	
natural	
political	

69

34 Outsourcing

Debate and decide on outsourcing strategy

1 **Work in small groups. Think of a definition of *outsourcing*, then look at the definition at the bottom of the page and see if you were correct.**

2 **In your groups, discuss which of these jobs could be moved from your country to a country with lower costs.**

- clothing manufacturing
- postal and courier services
- medical services
- office furniture and supplies
- banking and financial services

Listening

3 ((((34.1)))) **Enrico Milazzi is the Managing Director of an electronic components manufacturer in Italy. They have recently outsourced 80% of their production abroad. Listen to him describing his company's experience. What questions is he asked?**

4 **Decide if these statements are true (T) or false (F). Correct the false ones.**

1 Enrico needed to lower production costs.
2 They were able to buy a production plant with the latest and most efficient technology.
3 The labour force in Europe is cheaper than other areas.
4 Research and development remains in Italy.
5 Non-standard product requests and priority orders are still produced in the Italian factory.

Key language for outsourcing

We've {
relocated to …
outsourced our (payroll department) to …
offshored our (production) to …
moved our (customer support) to …
}

Why

We can focus on our core business.
We've saved on costs.
Labour is much cheaper.
There's a skilled, educated workforce.
It's increased jobs and wealth in the region.

Pros

It gives us the freedom to work when and where we want.
We have much higher productivity.
Experts work together across distances.
We've saved on offices and travel costs.
Time is saved on travel.
There's increased market opportunity globally.

Cons

There's been a loss of jobs locally.
The quality of service has dropped.
We've had supply-chain issues.
We needed to do a lot of retraining.

---

outsourcing: An arrangement in which work is done by people from outside your company, usually by a company that is expert in that type of work. This includes both foreign and domestic work and sometimes includes offshoring or relocating a business function to another country where costs are lower.

Pronunciation   *u* sounds

1 (((34.2))) **The letter *u* in English can be pronounced in several different ways. Listen and place these words in the correct column of the table below according to the *u* sounds.**

~~consume~~   educated   ~~focus~~   ~~fruit~~   include   juice   June   manufacture   produce   rule   supply support   Tunisia   usual

/ju:/	/u:/	/ə/
consume	fruit	focus

2 (((34.2))) **Listen again and practise saying the words.**

Get ready

5 **Complete the notes below with words from the box.**

provider   in-house   geopolitical   global   professionals   third

- Reliance on [1]................. parties
- Lower costs
- Work done faster through a [2]................. workforce
- Redundancies and demotivation caused by transferring jobs to other countries
- [3]................. risks
- Language differences and poor communication
- Lack of client focus from outsourcing [4].................
- Specialised skills
- Better availability of skilled [5].................
- Flexible labour
- Lack of [6]................. knowledge for business operations
- Cost efficiencies

6 **Work with a partner and decide if the points in Exercise 5 are benefits or drawbacks of outsourcing. Can you think of any others?**

Task

7 **Work in two groups, A and B. You work for a computer company based in San Francisco, US, and you're thinking about outsourcing your manufacturing and customer support centre to Bangalore, India.**

Group A: Decide why your manufacturing and customer support centre should be moved to Bangalore.

Group B: Decide why your manufacturing and customer support centre should remain in your own country.

8 **Now get together and hold a meeting on this subject. You may want to use the language in Units 25 and 30 to help you.**

Follow-up

9 **Does your company outsource any of its work? Do you think this is successful? What are the benefits and drawbacks for your company?**

10 **Would you be happy to move and work overseas? Which country would you prefer?**

The economy

1 The economy can be divided into three sectors:

Primary: agriculture and raw-material extraction
Secondary: manufacturing, construction
Tertiary: services

Describe these photos and say which sector of the economy each one relates to.

2 Discuss these questions.

1 In which sector is your country's economy most productive?
2 Is this situation changing?

Key language for talking about economic performance

currency
commodities
natural resources
energy: gas, oil, coal, nuclear, renewables
imports and exports
gross domestic product (GDP)
rate of inflation/taxation/unemployment
wealth and poverty, the gap between rich and poor
public spending
economic growth
trade agreements

Listening

3 (((35.1))) **Listen to an economist describing the economy of Australia. On the whole, does he paint a positive picture? Why?**

4 (((35.1))) **Listen again and decide if these statements are true (T) or false (F). Correct the false ones.**

1 Australia's economy has grown for the last 20 years.
2 The rate of inflation is higher than the rate of unemployment.
3 Australia produces more coal than it consumes.
4 It exports the majority of its agricultural produce.
5 The country is now manufacturing more than ever.
6 Finance and communications are the most significant parts of the service sector.

Get ready

5 **Match these definitions with words or phrases in the Key language section.**

1 Goods for sale brought into or sent out of a country
2 The amount the government spends on things such as health, education and defence
3 The money used in a country
4 Raw materials or agricultural produce that can be bought and sold, like coal or coffee
5 The percentage of the workforce without a job
6 Sources of energy that are not lost when used
7 The value of all the goods and services produced by a country in a year
8 The percentage that prices generally increase

6 **Work with a partner. Choose a country (not your own) and talk about it for one minute using the Key language.**

Pronunciation   Word stress

1 (((35.2))) **Listen and place these words in the correct column of the table below, according to their stress patterns.**

~~an export~~   to export   an increase   to increase   an import   to import

2 (((35.3))) **Listen and place these words in the correct column.**

commodities   economy   employment   government   industry   percentage

oO	Oo	oOo	oOoo	Ooo
	an export			

Task

7 **Make brief notes and prepare to give a short talk about your country's economy, including some or all of these topics.**

• Primary, secondary and tertiary sectors
• Inflation and unemployment
• Energy
• Currency and trade agreements
• Taxation
• Wealth and poverty

36 The environment

Talk about the effects of industry on the environment

Discuss how your business reacts to environmental problems

1 Look at the photos and say how the things in the box damage the environment.

Example: *Traffic causes air pollution and climate change.*

| traffic   factories   air travel   nuclear power plants   deforestation   shipping   burning coal |

2 What impact does your business have on the environment?

Key language for talking about the environment

Effects of pollution
to pollute the atmosphere/water/soil
to damage the ozone layer
to cause radioactivity
to make noise

Protecting the environment
to prevent climate change
to avoid wasting energy/paper
to use clean energy
to recycle waste
to be eco-friendly
to switch off electricity

to turn off water
to buy locally
to share cars
to use occupancy sensors
to control office heating/cooling
to use green transport

3 Match phrases from *Protecting the environment* in the Key language section with these pictures.

❶

❷

❸

❹

❺

❻

❼

Listening

4 (((36.1))) **Listen to part of a talk by a business environment consultant in which she describes ways companies can make themselves 'greener'. Which five ideas in Exercise 3 does she talk about?**

5 (((36.1))) **Listen again and answer these questions.**

1 According to the consultant, which two other benefits can businesses gain from becoming more environmentally friendly, apart from helping the environment?
2 What are 'occupancy sensors'?
3 What does the consultant suggest a company can offer employees who participate in car-sharing schemes?

Task

6 Work with a partner. Interview each other to find out about your companies' environmental performances.

ENVIRONMENTAL PERFORMANCE

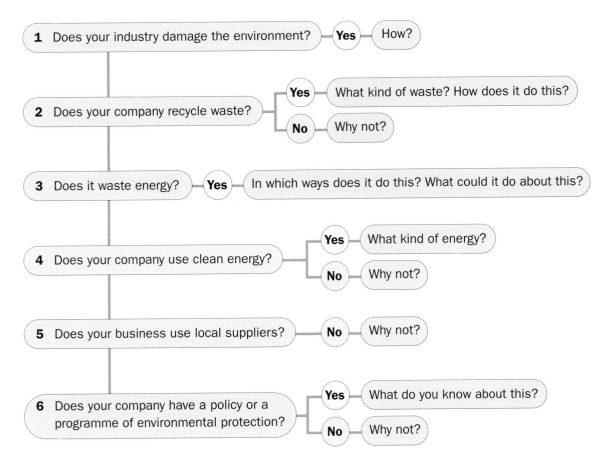

1 Does your industry damage the environment? — **Yes** — How?

2 Does your company recycle waste? — **Yes** — What kind of waste? How does it do this? / **No** — Why not?

3 Does it waste energy? — **Yes** — In which ways does it do this? What could it do about this?

4 Does your company use clean energy? — **Yes** — What kind of energy? / **No** — Why not?

5 Does your business use local suppliers? — **No** — Why not?

6 Does your company have a policy or a programme of environmental protection? — **Yes** — What do you know about this? / **No** — Why not?

Follow-up

7 How far do you agree with these statements?

- Fracking (hydraulic fracturing) should be illegal.
- Nuclear energy doesn't damage the ozone layer. We need more of it.
- The first responsibility of a company is to make a profit.
- Politicians aren't able to solve the world's environmental problems.

37

The competition

....

Discuss ways to compete

Analyse your competitors

1 Do you or your company sometimes prefer to buy the products or services of less famous names? Why?

2 Imagine you're helping a small business to enter a competitive market. Work with a partner and tick (✓) the relevant column to show how important you think each of these factors is.

	Essential	Important	Preferable	Not needed
1 Differentiate your products from those of the competition.				
2 Sell at a lower price.				
3 Identify a need and fill it.				
4 Get as much social media presence as possible.				
5 Understand the competition.				
6 Have a better-quality product or service than your competitors.				
7 Make a plan and stick to it.				
8 Make sure you're quick to market.				

Listening

LUSH
FRESH HANDMADE COSMETICS

3 (((37.1))) When Mark and Mo Constantine opened the first Lush shop in the UK in 1994, few people thought that they would have any success against the giant multinational cosmetic companies. They now have 830 stores in 51 countries.

Listen to a market analyst talking about the reasons for their success. Which of the pieces of advice in the table in Exercise 2 is true for Lush?

4 (((37.1))) Listen again and decide if these sentences are true (T) or false (F). Correct the false ones.

1 There is a strong smell outside a Lush shop.
2 You can eat some of the store's products.
3 Lush sends catalogues direct to its customers.
4 Their prices are quite low.
5 The Constantines decided to copy their competitors.

Pronunciation   Weak forms 4

1 (((37.2))) Listen and identify the schwa /ə/ sound in these sentences. How many are there?

1 Their price is the same as ours.
2 The atmosphere is warmer and more welcoming than other shops.
3 Lush is very different from its competitors.
4 Our costs aren't as high as theirs.
5 Their market share is bigger than ours.

2 (((37.2))) Listen again and repeat the sentences.

Key language for talking about the competition

to be different from/to
to be the same as
a competitive market
to have a competitive advantage
to compete for a share of the market
to beat / differentiate from the competition
indirect competitors/competition
a threat / to threaten

to build a reputation through word of mouth
to be present in social media
to win a contract
to be weaker / stronger / more efficient / quicker to market
to offer lower prices / a better-quality product or service / a more attractive product
to be the most profitable

Get ready

5 Match the sentence halves.

1 Chocolate has several indirect
2 If we can differentiate from the competition,
3 Their competitive advantage
4 If we want to win the contract,
5 Their new products
6 They built their reputation
7 This product is the

a are a threat to our market share.
b competitors, such as crisps.
c is their highly skilled staff.
d through word of mouth.
e most profitable.
f we'll be able to offer a more attractive product.
g we'll have to offer a better service.

6 Compare these groups using comparatives and superlatives.

Example: 1 *A Kia is cheaper than a Volvo. A Ferrari is the most expensive.*

1 Volvo Ferrari Kia
2 8 pm 10 pm midnight
3 Republic of Korea Japan China
4 whisky wine beer
5 Lufthansa Ryanair Qantas
6 taxi train bicycle
7 mobile phone laptop computer desktop computer
8 Google Bing Yahoo!
9 solar energy nuclear energy fossil-fuel energy

Task

7 Work with a partner. How well do you know your competitors?

8 What do you think your company should do to improve this situation?

1 Who are they?	2 What are they like?	3 What are they offering?
• Who are your competitors? • Do you have the same customers? • Which competitors affect you more: those at home or abroad? • Do you also have indirect competitors?	• Which competitors are the biggest threat? • How big are they? • Are they growing or shrinking? Why? • What is their market share? • Which are the most profitable? Why?	• What's the difference between what you and your competitors are offering? • What's their policy on pricing?
4 Competitive advantage	5 In the public eye	6 Better or worse?
• Do they have a competitive advantage? • Do you have a competitive advantage?	• What's their reputation? • Do they promote themselves better than you? • Do they use digital technology better than you?	• In which ways are your competitors stronger than you? • In which ways are they weaker than you?

Cross-cultural communication

Talk about contrasting cultural language styles

1 Research has shown several significant differences in the ways cultures communicate. A failure to appreciate these differences can result in misunderstandings in international business. Apart from language differences, what kind of problems do you think people can have when communicating across cultures?

Get ready

2 Read the pairs of cultural communication styles (1–5). Do you associate certain countries with these characteristics?

1

A Group opinions	B Individual opinions
We agree … We all think …	I think … I don't know. I disagree.

2

A Indirect	B Direct
They prefer to use an indirect speaking style. It's not important to be so exact. They think that the listener is able to understand what they're trying to communicate from the situation. Words like *maybe* or *perhaps* are used to avoid possibly hurting the feelings of others. Would you like to invest in this project? Perhaps, we'll see.	The situation is not so important. When they mean 'no', they say 'no'! Would you like to invest in this project? No, thanks. It's not for us.

3

A Uncertainty is not a problem	B Avoid uncertainty
Things don't have to be black and white. They don't mind change. They're quite informal and generally have low stress levels. It sounds interesting. Let's risk it!	They like a lot of rules, laws and regulations and plan everything. They use words like *absolutely* and *certainly*. We must carry out a thorough analysis of all aspects before we decide to change.

4

A Elaborate style	B Brief style
They use rich language, lots of adjectives, exaggerations, idioms, metaphors, etc. Their first answer to a question often needs to be supported by other language Welcome, you have brought light to my house!	They just use the words that are necessary, no more. Hi, come in.

5	A Comfortable with formal language	B Uncomfortable with formal language
	They use very flexible language depending on participants in the conversation.	They prefer to see everybody as the same and generally don't use titles and formal language. They tend to use first names.
	We'd be very grateful for your assistance.	Can you help us?

In the UK and the USA, this means 'OK'.

In Japan, it means 'money'.

In Russia, it means 'zero'

But in Brazil, it's very rude!

Listening

3 (((38.1))) **Listen to five short examples of the styles in Exercise 2 and match them to A or B of each pair.**

Task

4 **Work with a partner or small groups. Look at the contrasting cultural language characteristics below and put a cross on the lines where you think your own culture(s) correspond(s). Compare and explain your answers.**

Group opinions ←————————→ Individual opinions

Indirect ←————————→ Direct

Uncertainty is not a problem ←————————→ Avoid uncertainty

Elaborate style ←————————→ Brief style

Comfortable with formal language ←————————→ Uncomfortable with formal language

5 **Discuss these questions about your communication styles.**

1 If you come from different cultures in your class, what differences do you think there are between your cultural communication styles?

2 If you all come from the same culture in your class, what differences do you think there are between your cultural communication style and those of others?

3 What advice would you give people trying to do business in your country?

4 How do you think you should modify your own communication style in business dealings with other cultures?

5 Do you agree with the saying 'When in Rome, do as the Romans do'? Why? / Why not?

6 Have you ever experienced 'culture shock' when visiting another country? Why?

39 Virtual teamwork

Talk about communicating online

Listening

1 Have you heard of 'virtual teams'? What do you think they are?

2 Read the definition at the bottom of page 81. Were you correct?

3 (((39.1))) Listen to the work experiences of Euan Van Reep and Danny Lee and complete these notes.

Euan Van Reep

Job: ¹...

- My office: ²...........................
- The website designed in:
  ³...........................
- Software developed in:
  ⁴...........................
- Methods of communication: –
  – ⁵........................... and ⁶...........................
  – ⁷........................... meeting with the team leader

---

Danny Lee

Job: ⁸...

- Head office: ⁹...........................
- Staff in: ¹⁰..........................., Malaysia
- Factory in: ¹¹..........................., Indonesia
- Methods of communication:
  – ¹²........................... and ¹³...........................
  – ¹⁴........................... systems and business trips

Key language for talking about virtual teams

Benefits

I have the freedom to work when and where I want.
There is a high level of individual job satisfaction.
Virtual teamwork can be very productive.
It's great when experts can work together across large distances.
We save a lot of money on offices and travel costs.
So much time is saved on travel.
As the team is global, there is an increased market opportunity.

Challenges

It's difficult to
{ build trust.
establish common goals.
ensure good communication and good practices.
manage problem-solving effectively.
manage people in different areas. }

The technology is changing continuously.
There can be a lot of misunderstanding with other members of the team.
We have some technical communication problems.
Different cultures have different work routines.

Get ready

4 Match the communication methods (1–7) with their definitions (a–g).

1 file sharing
2 video-chatting
3 social media
4 data conferencing
5 chat rooms
6 e-mailing
7 instant messaging

a a system for sending and receiving messages electronically over a computer network
b sharing computer data or space on a network
c participating in a webcam-based discussion with one or more people
d transmission of an electronic message over a computer network using software that immediately displays the message
e a branch of a computer system in which participants can engage in live discussions with one another
f sharing data interactively among several users in different locations
g online forms of communicating that any individual can employ, including blogs

5 Can you think of examples of the communication methods in Exercise 4?

Example: 2 *Skype*

Task

6 Complete the profile below about your job and describe it to your partner.

7 Now compare virtual work experiences with your partner. What do you think are the advantages and disadvantages of your experiences?

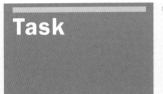

> Job: ....
>
> • My office: ....
> • Head office: ....
> • Other places: ....
>
> • Methods of communication:
>   ....
>   ....

Follow-up

8 There are 2.9 million full-time virtual workers in the US, and 13% of the working population of the EU works virtually. These numbers are growing every year. Discuss these questions.

1 Do you work in a virtual team? How do you feel about this?
2 Do you know anyone who works in a virtual team? What do they do?
3 Do any of your customers/suppliers use virtual teams? Are they successful?

> **virtual teams:** Groups of people working across boundaries of time, geography and organisation. This allows companies to use the best people for the job, wherever they are in the world.

1 **The purpose of the game is to win the most money from your investments. Work with a partner or in small groups. You have €100,000 to invest, in two lots of €50,000.**

Read about the following investment opportunities and decide how you're going to invest your first €50,000. You can invest in as many of the companies as you want, but you must invest all of the money!

Phonecom
This was once a state monopoly, but was privatised eight years ago. It now faces much more competition than before.
150c a share

Fulchester Football Club
This is one of Europe's biggest soccer clubs. Second in the championship last year, it has a large merchandising operation.
100c a share

Bridge Automobiles
A small manufacturer, Bridge has recently developed a car which runs efficiently on natural gas.
50c a share

PH Pharmaceuticals
PH is one of the world's largest manufacturers of prescription drugs and has been involved in several mergers with other large drug companies.
1,000c a share

Tower Insurance
This is an old insurance company, established in 1792. It is one of the top five insurance companies in the country.
250c a share

Palace Leisure
This is a medium-sized company with several cinemas, casinos and hotels around the world. It is now expanding into the tourist business – selling holidays.
150c a share

PB Oil
This company drills for oil and gas in about 20 countries and owns 28,000 petrol stations worldwide.
1,500c a share

National Bank
Investment account with fixed-rate annual interest: *5%*

Listening

2 (((40.1))) **It's now three months later. Listen to the financial report and take notes of your new share values. Then calculate your current position.**

	New price	Profit/loss
Phonecom		
Fulchester Football Club		
Bridge Automobiles		
PH Pharmaceuticals		
Tower Insurance		
Palace Leisure		
PB Oil		

3 You now have another €50,000 to invest. Read about some new investment opportunities. If you wish, you may also sell some of your old stock to buy more.

CITY TIPS

Tesbury Supermarkets
People will always have to eat, and now there's news that the retail chain is starting to perform well in Asia.
150c a share

Laura Bentley
The fashion and interior design company now looks comfortable after closing down its US operations three years ago. It has just opened five more stores in Europe.
50c a share

NSU Bank
NSU is making profits of €6m a day after attracting customers to its new cheap savings products. This bank's problems look a thing of the past.
500c a share

Guilders
The past three years have been hard for this fund-management company, but with their investment performance now greatly improved, it looks like they have turned the corner.
700c a share

Blue K Mines
This Australian company has a mining cost of 225c per gram of gold. But the price of gold is currently 300c a gram. That means profit.
10c a share

Rockit Recording
The global music market is getting smaller, but this small recording company has some good niche opportunities, with its country, reggae and heavy-metal music contracts. It has also recently started making films.
50c a share

BexBio
Some of the world's biggest names in drugs have been developed by this company. The news is they have now developed a very effective flu treatment.
1,000c a share

Mediamix
After its headache with the internet, it seems this media giant is now concentrating on its core business of television. A brighter future?
200c a share

Listening

4 (((40.2))) It's three months later. Listen to the latest financial report and take notes of your new share values. Then calculate your final position. If your investment isn't mentioned in the report, it stays unchanged.

	New price	Profit/loss
Fulchester Football Club		
Bridge Automobiles		
PB Oil		
Guilders		
Blue K Mines		
Rockit Recording		
BexBio		
Mediamix		

Turn to page 86 to check your score.

Activity files

Unit 11, Exercise 5

Student B

Make these calls.

1 You're calling the bank because your company paid a VAT bill at the bank on 4th April last year, but now your accountant says the tax authorities have told him that it hasn't been paid and that you'll receive a fine. You've checked the account online, and the money didn't leave your account. You have a paper receipt of the VAT demand stamped and dated by the bank.

2 You're a customer of Happy Holidays Travel Agency. You recently returned from a skiing holiday in France. The 'three-star' hotel you stayed in was extremely low quality in terms of hygiene and food, and you had to pay extra for breakfast, which wasn't in the agreement. Unfortunately, after one week of your two-week holiday, your son broke his leg and you had to return home. Now the agency is refusing to reimburse you the money for the second week, even though you know your room was occupied by other guests.

Receive these calls.

3 You work for Multiparts Engineering Ltd. You'll receive a call about a quality problem. You haven't had any quality problems in your factory for a year.

4 You work for Easyran Air Customer Service department. You'll receive a call from a customer who wants to be reimbursed for excess baggage. It's not your company's policy to refund excess baggage charges if they're correctly applied at the point of departure.

Unit 20, Exercise 3

Student A

Describe this graph to Student B.

Listen to Student B and complete the chart that they describe.

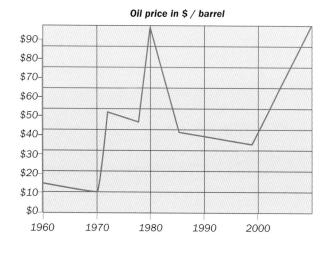

Oil price in $ / barrel

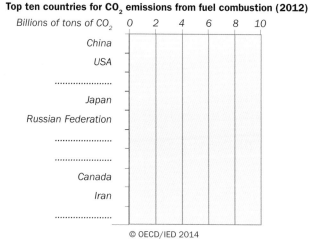

Top ten countries for CO_2 emissions from fuel combustion (2012)

© OECD/IED 2014

Unit 22, Exercise 6

Seller A

Product	Last year's sales	Sales target	Your forecast	Reasons for forecast
A online sales of nappies and baby goods	[1]............	€160,000 gross	[2]............	recession in Western economies means that parents are buying cheaper brands
B [3]............ printer	€130,000	[4]............	€220,000	• increase in [5]............ use of 3D printers • more retailers are selling them

Unit 8, Exercise 4

Student B

FedEx

Background

Can you see the arrow in the logo?
Founded 1971 in Little Rock, Arkansas, by Frederick W. Smith.
1.2 billion packages now shipped annually by FedEx.

Operations facts

Daily miles travelled by the FedEx air fleet:	500,000
Delivery vans in the FedEx fleet:	43,000
Planes in the FedEx fleet:	654
% of shipped packages lost by FedEx:	0.55%

Employees

Number of full-time FedEx employees:	300,000
Highest FedEx employee salary (IT Manager):	$123,000
Lowest FedEx employee (Customer Service Representative):	$10.42/hour

Finance

Annual FedEx revenue:	$39.3 billion
Highest historic stock price (Feb 17, 2007):	$120.97
Lowest historic stock price (May 6, 1980):	$2.50

Source: http://www.statisticbrain.com 2012

Unit 13, Exercise 9

Interview 2

1 Why / choose your course at college/ university?
2 Why / want this job?
3 have a job at the moment?
   Yes → Why / thinking about leaving / this job?
   No → Tell me / why / leave / last job.
4 Could / describe what / do in your last/current job?
5 What experience / have doing [*job area*]?
6 Describe a situation in which you led / worked in a team.
7 prefer / work in a team or by yourself?
8 Tell me about a time / worked with / interpreting / presenting data.
9 How / you organise your time at work?
10 What most interests you about your work?
11 What / your weaknesses?
12 Who else / you applied to?
13 What / you expect to be doing in five years' time?
14 Tell me about a time when you had to respond to a crisis.
15 What / be your greatest achievement?
16 How / prefer to communicate at work?
17 you think / good at dealing with people?

Write three questions of your own.

18 ....
19 ....
20 ....
21 have / any questions?

Unit 40

Scores

If you've made a profit of:
- more than €150,000, maybe you should start playing the real thing.
- between €100,000 and €150,000, how are you going to spend it all?
- between €50,000 and €100,000, you've made some wise investments.
- less than €50,000, don't worry – the important thing is not to lose money.

If you've made a loss of:
- less than €50,000, put the rest in the bank and go back to work.
- more than €50,000, don't worry – what's money compared to health and love?

Unit 13, Exercise 9

Interview 1

1 What can / tell me about yourself?
2 Why / want to work for us?
3 What / know about our company?
4 have a job at the moment?
  Yes → Why / thinking about leaving / this job?
  No → Tell me / why / leave / last job.
5 When / you be available to start work?
6 Could you tell me about your experience in [job area].
7 attended any training courses in [job area]?
8 Why / think we / choose you for this job?
9 not think you're too old/young for this job?
10 Can / tell me what / like to do in your spare time?

11 What / think of your present/last boss?
12 What / your strong points?
13 Tell me about a time when you / deal with a problem at work.
14 What / think / right salary for this job?
15 What are the important trends in this industry?
16 think you're good at leading people? Why?
17 When / the last time you got angry?

Write three questions of your own.
18 ....
19 ....
20 ....
21 have any questions you / like / ask me?

Unit 20, Exercise 3

Student B

Describe this chart to Student A.

Listen to Student A and complete the graph that they describe.

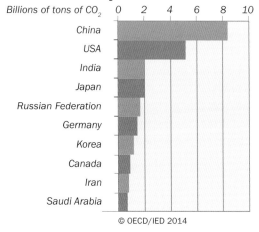

Top ten countries for CO_2 emissions from fuel combustion (2012)

© OECD/IED 2014

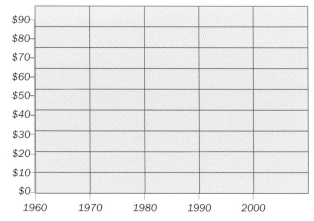

Oil price in $ / barrel

Unit 22, Exercise 6

Seller B

Product	Last year's sales	Sales target	Your forecast	Reasons for forecast
A online sales of [1]............	€150,000	[2]............	€120,000	recession in Western economies means that [3]............
B 3D printer	[4]............	€260,000 gross	[5]............	• increase in domestic use of 3D printers • more retailers are selling them

Audio scripts

Audio 1.1

Operator: Telstram, good morning.

Peter: Good morning, I'm calling about the advertisement I saw on *The Province* site for sales executives. Could I speak to Tina Fowler, please?

Operator: Hold the line, please. I'll try to connect you.

Tina: Hello?

Peter: Hello, this is Peter Carson. Could I speak to Ms Fowler, please?

Tina: Speaking! What can I do for you, Mr Carson?

Peter: Oh, good morning … I'm calling about the advertisement you placed on *The Province* website …

Tina: … for sales executives …

Peter: Exactly.

Tina: … and you're interested in applying.

Peter: Yes.

Tina: Good, well, can I ask … um … do you have any experience in sales?

Peter: Yes, I'm currently working as an area sales rep for PTK Foods in Montreal and—

Tina: Sorry to interrupt, Mr Carson, but I think we stated in our ad that we were looking for sales executives with technical experience.

Peter: Right, yes, but I've only been working for PTK since 2011, and I have, in fact, a lot of experience in your field. I was a salesman for one of your competitors – Orax – for five years before this job, a year of which was in Hamburg.

Tina: Oh, so you can speak German, then?

Peter: Yes, quite well. Anyway, my roots are really in IT, and I'm interested in getting back into it.

Tina: I see. Well, do you have any business qualifications?

Peter: Yes, I have a Bachelor's degree in business studies from Toronto University.

Tina: Well, that all sounds very interesting, Mr Carson. Now, we're getting very near to the closing date for applications, so do you think you could get your CV to us by the end of the week?

Peter: Sure, I can e-mail it to you this afternoon.

Tina: Fine, and can I have your phone number in case there's a problem?

Peter: Yeah, I'll give you my cell – it's 09435 683927.

Tina: 09435 683927. OK.

Peter: Well, I look forward to hearing from you, Ms Fowler.

Tina: OK, thank you for calling. Bye.

Audio 1.2

1 I was born in Paris.
2 He's qualified as an engineer.
3 She's got a degree in economics.
4 He resigned on Friday.
5 I'm currently working as a flight attendant.
6 She went out at eight.
7 He sent in his CV to the company.

Audio 2.1

1 Well, the main thing I aim to do in my job is to reduce the amount of time that my boss, the Finance Director, spends on meetings and talking to people. So I'm filtering quite a lot of the time. Then I have to help him prepare presentations for internal meetings, and he sometimes 'lends' me to the Managing Director to do the same thing. Another important part of my job is to liaise with Human Resources concerning hiring new personnel in the finance area.

2 That's the title on my job description, but it's had other titles in the past – but whatever you call it, you're not a very popular figure with the workforce. It's my job to analyse other people's jobs in the company, and in particular, I examine the process needed to produce something. So I have to study the old procedures and the current organisation of a job. Then I try to find another, better way of doing it. Then, of course, I have to report to my boss on the new procedure, and if he agrees, we'll change it. I'm also responsible for co-ordinating other people if I'm in charge of a project. At the moment, we're trying to reduce the number of …

3 The main purpose of my job is to improve the effectiveness of our machinery on the production line. I also have to set up and follow up on various sub-projects. At the moment, I'm arranging teamwork in the plant. Then I'll have to follow up on their performances.

Audio 2.2

1 She has to hire more personnel.
2 What's the main purpose of your job?
3 I have to deal with problems that come up every day, although I don't always manage to solve them.
4 This involves working with three other colleagues.
5 It's my job to analyse other people's jobs.
6 I've got to write an analysis of his job.
7 He said he's bought a new suit.
8 The company has more than two thousand employees worldwide.

Audio 3.1

Ric: So how was the trip?

Anna: Oh, the course was OK, but the journey was a nightmare.

Ric: Why?

Anna: Well, I wanted to leave Milan at eight in the evening, arrive in London about ten and get to the hotel by midnight.

Ric: But you didn't …

Anna: No. First of all, there was that public transport strike, so I got stuck in traffic in my car for about half an hour trying to get to the airport. Then I parked my car in the airport car park and rushed off to catch the plane.

Ric: Don't tell me there was a plane strike as well …

Anna: No, no, but after all that rush, we took off an hour late. That's not all, though – but this time it was my fault. We landed at Gatwick and I went to the station, but I got on the wrong train. Fortunately, I realised almost straight away, so I got off at the next station and went back to Gatwick. But by this time, the last train to Twickenham had left, and I was starting to feel quite stressed and sorry for myself.

Ric: Yeah, I bet.

Anna: Anyway, I decided to take a cab.

Ric: Why didn't you just check in at a hotel in Gatwick?

Anna: I was determined to get to the hotel in Twickenham. I had to be at the training course early the next morning. So, anyway, I got in a taxi at the airport and asked the driver to take me to Twickenham. You'll never guess how much it was – 70 pounds! But I had to agree – what else could I do?

Ric: Yeah.

Anna: Well, I eventually got to the hotel – you know, it took me longer to get from the airport to the hotel than from Milan to Gatwick – and by now it was half past one in the morning. I thought that was it when I got to the hotel, but the receptionist said they hadn't received any confirmation of the booking and …

Ric: And …

Anna: … and the hotel was full.

Ric: Oh great!

Anna: Yeah. I was trying to stay calm. I said I'd sent a confirmation of the booking, or rather Luisa had sent one for me, by e-mail. She said they'd had some trouble with their computer and that she was sorry, but she couldn't give me a room. Well, I just went crazy at this point and threatened to cancel the whole deal with their hotel – which, of course, I couldn't, by the way! – but anyway, that seemed to have the effect I was looking for and she gave me the presidential suite!

Ric: You're joking!

Anna: No, we were quite friendly after that.

Ric: It just shows what complaining can do … sometimes.

Anna: Yes, sometimes.

Audio 3.2

arrived   asked   decided   delayed   landed   looked   missed   parked   realised   received   rushed   seemed   stayed   threatened   visited   waited   wanted   worked

Audio 4.1

Interviewer: Alex, can you tell me how you spend most of your income?

Alex: Yeah, sure. We've got a house and we owe about 200,000 dollars on that. Paying off the mortgage costs us around 1,400 dollars a month, so that's the biggest single expense we have. Then there are living expenses like the gas and electricity bills, the local services tax, the shopping … we spend at least 200 dollars a week in the supermarket.

Pilar: We also have a daughter at university, so we have to pay the fees for that and her expenses.

Interviewer: What about a car?

Alex: Oh yes, we own two cars. We need them for our work, and it also means that we can lend the children a car if they ask, which they usually do, especially at weekends.

Interviewer: So do you manage to save much from your salaries at the end of the month?

Alex: You must be joking!

Pilar: Oh, come on, we save a bit for our holidays.

Alex: Yeah, a few dollars, I suppose.

Interviewer: You have your own business. Why don't you give yourselves a pay rise?

Pilar: Well, any profits we make we tend to put back into the company for now. We're trying to make the business grow.

Audio 4.2

right, married

Audio 4.3

agree, borrow, credit, free, hundred, real, right, wrong

Audio 5.1

Interviewer: What is the 'five whys' approach to problem-solving, Maxine?

Maxine: Toyota first developed this tool for solving problems in production. It's simple – you try to get to the cause of a problem by asking a series of *why* questions. Often just asking one *why* question won't get you to the real root of a problem – the answer to the first *why* can suggest another *why*, and the answer to the second *why* suggests a third, etc. First, you look at the end result of a problem and then work back until you get to the root cause. For example, let's take this European electronics company, company X. I'll start and you ask the *why* questions.

Interviewer: OK.

Maxine: Sales are down at company X.

Interviewer: Why are sales down?

Maxine: Because their prices have increased.

Interviewer: Why have their prices increased?

Maxine: Because of their increased costs.

Interviewer: Why have their costs increased?

Maxine: Because they only buy their supplies from the USA, and the dollar–euro exchange rate is very poor now.

Interviewer: So, why do they only buy their supplies from the USA?

Maxine: They've always bought them from there because they get good-quality components on time.

Interviewer: Why haven't they looked for other suppliers who could offer the same at a lower price?

Maxine: They haven't had time to do the research.

Interviewer: OK, so it seems they have to organise themselves to look for an alternative supplier when the exchange rate is bad.

Maxine: Yes, I'd agree. So you see, we got to the bottom of the problem very quickly. Sometimes, of course, things can be more complicated, and you need to use other tools like root-cause or cause-and-effect analysis or …

Audio 5.2

1 Why don't you try again?
2 Yes, I'd agree.
3 They've always bought them from there.
4 Since it was so expensive, we didn't buy it.
5 You shouldn't waste time with that.
6 I'll let you know tomorrow.

Audio 6.1

Waiter: Good evening, do you have a reservation?
Man: I'm afraid not.
Waiter: No problem, for how many?
Man: Just a table for two, please.

*****

Waiter: Are you ready to order?
Woman: Yes, I think so.
Waiter: Would you like a starter?
Woman: Yes, please. I'll have the baked aubergine.
Waiter: Certainly.
Man: Is the mackerel fresh?
Waiter: Of course, sir.
Man: I mean, it hasn't been frozen?
Waiter: No, sir – fresh today.
Man: I'd like that, then, please.
Waiter: The main course?
Woman: What would you recommend?
Waiter: The sea bass is particularly good today – fresh, of course.
Woman: OK, I'll have that, but without the aubergine.
Waiter: Yes, we can do that.
Man: And I'll have the stir-fried beef.
Waiter: And one stir-fried beef. What would you like to drink?
Woman: White wine, Stephen? What do you think?
Man: I'd just like water.
Waiter: Shall I bring you the wine list?
Woman: Do you have a dry house white?
Waiter: Yes, madam, we have a Pinot Grigio.
Woman: Fine, a half bottle of that, please.
Waiter: Certainly, and will that be sparkling water for you, sir?
Man: No, half a litre of still, please.
Waiter: Would you like to order dessert now?
Woman: No, thanks. Maybe later.

*****

Man: I thought you were vegetarian, Lucy.
Woman: I am, but I eat fish.
Man: Oh, is that possible?
Woman: What?
Man: To be a vegetarian and eat fish.
Woman: Well, not strictly speaking, but I like fish and so sometimes I just …

Audio 6.2

although, clothes, other, that, the, then, there, together
both, healthy, mouth, something, teeth, thank, thing, think

Audio 7.1

1 **Man:** Hello, Ms Kay's office.
  Giselle: Good morning, this is Giselle Schneider from JT Zurich. I'm calling about Ms Kay's arrangements for the conference this week.
  Man: I'm afraid Ms Kay's not here at the moment. Could I help?
  Giselle: Yes, could you give her a message, please?
  Man: Certainly, go ahead.
  Giselle: Right, her hotel reservation for Thursday and Friday at the Rex Hotel has been changed to the Marriott Hotel in Talstrasse. It's a better hotel and very near the conference centre. I hope this is OK.
  Man: I'm sure that won't be a problem. Was there anything else?
  Giselle: No, that's all, thanks.
  Man: OK, I'll let her know as soon as I can. Bye!
  Giselle: Thank you. Goodbye.

2 This is a message for Mr Rose from Charles Becman, that's Charles Becman, B-E-C-M-A-N, at United Tools. There's a problem with two of your deliveries: first, delivery GD67PK still hasn't arrived. We've already talked about this, how urgent this is. If you can't deliver it by Friday the 21st, we'll have to cancel and find another supplier. Then, delivery reference FP56DT, which arrived on Thursday, is incomplete. The order stated 15 drills, but we only received 13. Please call me back on 01342 599864 as soon as you can.

3 **Emily:** Customer services, how can I help you?
Martin: Hello, is that Phoebe Webber?
Emily: No, this is Emily. Who's calling, please?
Martin: This is Portslade Mechanics. Can I speak to Miss Webber?
Emily: I'm afraid she's not in at the moment.
Martin: Can I leave a message for her?
Emily: Sure, what is it?
Martin: Can you tell her her car won't be ready till next Friday because we've found more problems with it. It needs a new gearbox. I've prepared the estimate. It's about a thousand pounds.
Emily: Oh dear. I think you'll have to speak to her about this.
Martin: Yeah, I know. Can you ask her to call me on 01554 623090? OK?
Emily: All right – can you give me your name and e-mail address?
Martin: My name's Martin Spanner, e-mail portmech@ freestyle.co.uk. That's P-O-R-T-M-E-C-H-at-F-R-E-E-S-T-Y-L-E-dot-co-dot-UK.
Emily: OK, got it.
Martin: Right, bye!
Emily: Bye!

Audio 8.1

Suchin: Good morning, everybody, my name's Suchin Bak and I'm Customer Services Manager for this region. The purpose of this talk this morning is to explain the customer-complaints procedure. It's very important that you have a clear idea of this, so if you have any questions, please feel free to interrupt as we go along. All right?
Now, I've divided up the presentation into three parts. First of all, we'll look at our first response to complaints according to how we receive them – by phone, by e-mail, etc. – and then I'll show you the standard steps we take to address each complaint. Finally, we'll do some practice situations to see how you deal with them.
Right, let's start by looking at how we receive complaints. As you can see from this diagram, customers can complain face to face or by e-mail or …

* * * * *

So, we've seen how we get complaints; now let's move on to the steps you take in order to deal with each complaint. I must emphasise that these are not suggestions for steps, they are the only way you are allowed to answer. Let's go into these steps in more detail now. First of all, you ask …

* * * * *

I think you're ready now to face some complaints, so let's go on to see how much you've learnt. There are some situations described in these envelopes – these are real customer complaints that we've received in the last 12 months – and I'd like you to work in small groups and come up with answers as to how you're going to deal with each one …

* * * * *

Right, good. Now, we're running out of time, so to summarise the main points from today, first you must always …

* * * * *

I hope that's given you a clear picture of our procedures for handling customer complaints. Are there any more questions before we break for lunch?

Audio 8.2

1 These are not suggestions for steps, they are the only way you are allowed to answer.
2 I don't want to lower some of our prices, I want to lower all of our prices.
3 As you can see from the graph, sales didn't go down in June, they went up.

Audio 8.3

1 **A:** James has gone to Detroit.
  B: No, he hasn't gone to Detroit, he's gone to Chicago.
2 **A:** Did you call on Wednesday or Thursday?
  B: I called on Wednesday and Thursday.
3 **A:** You haven't finished the report.
  B: I have finished the report.

Audio 9.1

Kurt: As you know, JLB has been in financial difficulty for some time now, and the banks are knocking on our door. I'm sure you all agree that this is a situation that can't go on – we must do something about it, and we must do it fast.
First of all, let me give you some background information on why I think we got ourselves into this trouble in the first place. Ten years ago, JLB was a company which was admired, we were profitable, everything was looking good. But then something happened: we lost sight of our original goals, the company …

* * * * *

Now we come to what I think is one of the real roots of our problems. *Let's look at this question of company assets in more detail, in particular machinery. Our yard here is full of machinery that we're repairing – and yes, I'll admit that we are good at repairing broken and old machinery – but our core business is construction, not machinery maintenance. Or it should be! If we look at one of our competitors – Watson's, for example – in November last year, we had 140 items of machinery on site, whereas they had just 30! Yes, 30! We had more or less the same number of contracts, but compared with them, we had nearly five times the amount of machinery. Why? What's the point? It's just a cost! That machinery is not working for us. Watson's buy new machinery for a job, then, when the job's finished, they sell it immediately … and it makes sense for us to do the same. So here's proposal number one: I strongly suggest we sell 60% of our machinery assets as soon as possible, and with the revenue from that, we invest in areas that can really help us grow the business. What are these areas? Well, let's move on to see what …*

Audio 10.1

A: What did you do at the weekend?
B: I stayed at home.
A: Really? Didn't you go out at all?
B: Well, we went shopping, but nothing else. It was OK, quite relaxing. What about you?
A: We went to the beach at Conil. It was beautiful, we swam for hours.
B: Did you? Nice. Do you think that's the best beach in that area?
A: I think it probably is, and I don't know why, but it's not so crowded at the weekends.
B: Yes … the last time we went to Conil, there was hardly anybody there. It was perfect.

Audio 10.2

1 **A:** I'm going to Vietnam in July.
  B: Really?
2 **A:** I'm not speaking at the conference tomorrow.
  B: Aren't you?
3 **A:** He's my boss.
  B: Is he?
4 **A:** The hotel's full.
  B: Is it?
5 **A:** I work for Honda.
  B: Do you?
6 **A:** She doesn't work here any more.
  B: Doesn't she?

Audio 11.1

Hina: Moshi moshi.
John: Good morning, may I speak to Ms Sato, please?
Hina: Yes, speaking. Who's calling, please?
John: This is John Fletcher from IPQ in London.
Hina: Oh, good evening, Mr Fletcher, or perhaps it's good morning for you?
John: Yes, it's nine thirty in the morning here. What time is it there?
Hina: Six thirty p.m.
John: Oh sorry, it's a bit late.
Hina: No problem, I'm still working.
John: OK, well, I'm calling about the programme for Mr Ito's visit to London next month. Originally, the plan was for Mr Ito to meet the directors on Tuesday the 10th, but we've hit a snag on that since we've—
Hina: Sorry, Mr Fletcher, I don't follow you. Could you speak a little more slowly, please? You're calling about Mr Ito's visit to London …

John: Yes, the meeting with the directors on the 10th, something's come up.

Hina: Sorry, what do you mean?

John: I mean there's a problem with the date of the meeting.

Hina: Oh, I see.

John: The programme that we sent you said Mr Ito will meet the directors on Tuesday …

Hina: Uh-huh.

John: … and visit the factory on Wednesday.

Hina: And the factory visit on Wednesday, yes.

John: Well, since some of the directors couldn't come to the meeting on Tuesday, because they'll be abroad, we'd like to arrange the factory visit for Tuesday, and the meeting with the directors on Thursday at two in the afternoon.

Hina: Ah, I see, so what you're saying is that the new programme is for Mr Ito to visit the factory on Tuesday the 10th of March and meet the directors on Thursday the 12th.

John: Exactly, but the meeting would be at two in the afternoon, not ten in the morning as it said in the programme.

Hina: OK, well, I don't think that will be a problem, but I need to check with Mr Ito first and get back to you. Could you confirm the new arrangements by e-mail, please?

John: Yes, sure, I'll send you an e-mail right away.

Hina: Yes, please, and I'll check with Mr Ito. Was there anything else?

John: No, that's it.

Hina: Right, thank you, Mr Fletcher.

John: Thank you, Hina, goodbye.

Hina: Bye.

Audio 12.1

Manager: Right, let's sort out my 'to do' list on a Priority Grid.

Assistant: Oh yes, OK. So that's 'important and urgent' …

Manager: Yes, then 'important but not urgent' … 'urgent but unimportant' …

Assistant: … and 'unimportant and not urgent'.

Manager: Right. So first, 'important and urgent'. Autogrill's Distribution Manager wants me to call him back, so I'll do that as soon as I've finished this. We've got to keep him happy.

Assistant: There's also next week's presentation to think about – that could take hours.

Manager: Yes, true, I can't leave it to the last minute. Also, today, I have to confirm our place in the Hong Kong Trade Fair in June.

Assistant: Yes.

Manager: Those are the most urgent, I'd say. So now 'important but not urgent' – there are quite a few things here, I think. I've got to plan next season's marketing campaign – that starts in two months.

Assistant: And I've got a list of potential customers here you have to call.

Manager: OK, and then I need to draw up a schedule for the software training course.

Assistant: OK … also Jack Petersen, the new Assistant Product Manager, says he wants to talk to you about his idea for a new product – he keeps asking me when you're free.

Manager: All right, but put him in the next category, 'urgent but not important'. Also, one of our suppliers wants to talk to me about prices – that's urgent for him, but it can wait as far as I'm concerned. Um … finally, 'not important and not urgent'. IT want me to clear my e-mail inbox, but I could waste a lot of time doing that. I'll do it another day. Then I have to wash the car … but I've seen dirtier cars!

Audio 12.2

/aɪ/	time	decide, price, priority, right
/eɪ/	main	campaign, delay, straight, waste
/əʊ/	go	know, most, slow, so
/eə/	fair	dare, prepare, share, their
/ɪə/	near	beer, dear, gear, here

Audio 13.1

1 **Interviewer:** Come in, Ms Budka. Have a seat.

Candidate: Thank you.

Interviewer: First of all, what can you tell us about yourself?

Candidate: Well, I graduated from the University of Warsaw four years ago, and since then, I've been working in a supporting role for front-office staff at Peel's Bank. I think I'm ready now to move on to a position with closer relations with the customer, in a bank such as this one.

Interviewer: I see. Tell us what you know about our bank.

Candidate: I know you're well established both at home and abroad, specialising mainly in trading, securities and asset management. You have a good reputation among my colleagues and customers. You're tough competitors. Your website says you value …

2 **Interviewer:** Come in, Mr Edmondson. Take a seat, please.

Candidate: Thank you, and may I say how great you look!

Interviewer: Thanks … um, first of all, what do you know about our bank?

Candidate: Er, I know it's Swiss and it's got an office here in Zagreb.

Interviewer: Yes … well, we're one of the largest banks of our kind, specialising in trading, securities and asset management, and for the last five years …

* * * * *

Interviewer: Can you tell us who else you've applied to?

Candidate: Yes, but before I answer that, could I ask you something?

Interviewer: Sure, go ahead.

Candidate: Would I have my own office?

Interviewer: I'm afraid I couldn't answer that at the moment. Can we get back to the question of where else you've …

Audio 14.1

Interviewer: Akma, you communicate with a lot of people in your job, don't you?

Akma: Yes, I do.

Interviewer: Could you tell us who you communicate with, both inside and outside your company, and what you usually talk about?

Akma: If you mean inside my company, RP Consulting, then I speak to my colleagues, who are either the people who report to me or my bosses. With my reports, I discuss projects and ask them to do specific tasks.

Interviewer: What about other companies in the group – do you have any contact with them?

Akma: Occasionally, yes, we discuss things we have in common.

Interviewer: And outside the company?

Akma: Outside I have a lot of contacts, with the clients first of all – I speak to their HR departments.

Interviewer: Who do you talk to there?

Akma: The HR Director usually, or some specialists they have. We talk about the proposals we've made and the progress made on projects. I also sometimes talk to the General Manager or the CEO and to the Purchasing Department.

Interviewer: About?

Akma: In the Purchasing Department?

Interviewer: Yes.

Akma: About prices.

Interviewer: Right. Anybody else external to the company?

Akma: Yes, um, let's see, I talk to journalists, who ask me about trends in rewards and HR in general, and … institutions – I mean associations – and, er, … politicians too – I was talking to one last week about a research survey we did at RP. And I talk to publishers, like you.

Audio 14.2

1 I talked to Jack about the date.
2 They asked us for more money.
3 His boss shouted at him when he made a mistake.
4 I reminded her of the appointment.
5 They blamed me for the mistake.
6 We warned them about the danger.

Audio 15.1

Yusuf: Organisational structures can be flat or they can be hierarchical. Hierarchical organisations have lots of levels of management. This is typical of very large organisations. Flat structures have fewer levels of management, and people generally have more control over their work.

Common ways of organising companies include functional structures and business-unit structures. Functional structures group people together according to their jobs, so you might have, for example, Production, Marketing, Sales, Finance, Research and Development, Human Resources, IT and Distribution as separate departments. Business-unit structures are built around a particular product or service. So, for example, a media company might be divided into business units around TV, online and print media, with each unit having its own production and marketing staff.

Audio 15.2

charge, hierarchy, marketing
confirm, early, virtual, work, world
law, reports, resources, walk
parent, shares

Audio 16.1

1 Well, this is sold in tubes or jars. The tubes weigh 250 grams, and the jars are 500 grams. We've recently transferred production to a new factory, and we've had problems maintaining the characteristics of the product that we want. This is always a problem, or a challenge, I should say, in the food industry. Anyway, it needs to be a little creamier for the German market. The cap is a new feature developed in the US. You just screw it down more to open it.
2 With this account, you get an excellent interest rate, but you have to give 60 days' notice of withdrawal. Interest is paid either monthly or yearly, before tax. It's up to you to take care of that. The account is viewable online. This means you can check it or send us queries any time you want.
3 The beauty of this one is that it offers a complete package for only 49 euros per year: it includes anti-virus, anti-spyware, anti-spam, a two-way firewall and browser protection, but also parental control, online storage, online back-up and identity protection. You also get free online assistance if you have problems.
4 This is a 3D lens that fits onto a 2D camera, so you can shoot in 3D. It just clicks in here like that, then you need a few moments to set it up. If you go to our site, there's a video which explains how to get the best results from your 3D filming. It only weighs half a kilo, is powered by the same battery as the 2D version and the retail price is very reasonable, just $950.

Audio 16.2

We take care of all the problems.
Businesses are interested in this.
It's for opening the packaging.

Audio 16.3

for us – Is that for us?
there is – There is a video which explains everything.
more apples – We need more apples.
there are – There are jars of 500 grams.
far is – How far is it?
near enough – It's near enough.

Audio 17.1

1 First of all, the plastic is heated to 230 degrees Centigrade.
2 Then the liquid is forced into moulds.
3 Once the plastic has cooled in the moulds, the Lego bits are emptied into containers.
4 After that, the containers are transported by robots to the assembly line.
5 Next, the toys are packed on the assembly line.
6 Finally, robots prepare the boxes for distribution.

Audio 18.1

Alex: Hello, are you from Toyota?
Kaito: No, Nissan, and you?
Alex: I work for Fiat, I'm an engineer.
Kaito: Are you? So am I. I've just been to the presentation on electric cars. It's not really my field, but it was interesting.
Alex: Yes, it's definitely the future, I think. So you work on traditional engines?
Kaito: Yes, high-performance cars mainly.
Alex: Oh, I used to work for Ferrari.
Kaito: Really, did you? Where were you based? In Modena?
Alex: No, I was in the UK. Actually, I'm quite interested in getting back into that area. High-performance engines, I mean.
Kaito: Well, I know Mercedes are recruiting engineers at the moment.
Alex: Are they?
Kaito: Yes, I don't know what they're looking for exactly, but …
Alex: No, it sounds very interesting … Mr Tanaka, if I've pronounced the name on your badge correctly?
Kaito: Tanaka, yes, but you can call me Kaito.
Alex: Nice to meet you, Kaito. I'm Alex, Alex Bianchi, and I could really do with a coffee. Would you like to join me?
Kaito: Yes, sure.
Alex: Good. Then I think I'll go and find the Mercedes stand. Would you know who …

Audio 18.2

1 I'm leaving tomorrow.
2 I went to school in Rome.
3 She can't do it.
4 I was staying at the Hotel Regent last year.
5 I haven't seen her yet.
6 She works for Bayer.
7 I have to go soon.
8 I didn't enjoy that.

Audio 18.3

A: I won a prize in the competition.
B: Really? Did you? So did I!

Audio 18.4

1 **A:** I'm lost!
   B: Really? Are you? So am I!
2 **A:** I was born on the 4th of April.
   B: Really? Were you? So was I!
3 **A:** Greta's staying at the Five Pines Hotel.
   B: Really? Is she? So am I!
4 **A:** She was at the presentation yesterday.
   B: Really? Was she? So was I!
5 **A:** I went to Acapulco on holiday last summer.
   B: Really? Did you? So did I!
6 **A:** I've got an old Jaguar Mark 2.
   B: Really? Have you? So have I!

Audio 19.1

Interviewer: Anita, you've launched lots of successful products, particularly in the food-and-drinks sector, I believe.
Anita: Well, they haven't all been a fantastic success – that would be impossible – but on the whole, they've done well, yes.
Interviewer: So what advice would you give somebody who wants to launch a new product or service?
Anita: First of all, you need to do market research. When you've done that, you have to come up with ideas for the new product and evaluate those ideas very carefully. Then of course you have to invest in the idea, or find investment for it.
Interviewer: OK, so let's say you've got a great idea and you've got the investment – what's next?

Anita: Before you start to develop, to create the product, you have to clearly define what it is, and what it isn't. You shouldn't try to please everybody with everything. Then when you've done that and you're happy with it, you can start to develop it. You mustn't go into full production, of course. I mean you should make some samples of the product and then test it on the market.

Interviewer: All right. So if that all goes well, then what?

Anita: Now you're ready for the launch. Some people think OK, we've done all the hard work, let's relax and see what happens. But actually you have to work very hard at this stage – start the conversation with the customers, promote the product in multiple channels – on the web, through social networking and so on. You've got to get your message across and make sure that you're underlining the product's advantages and benefits. Then you can sit back and cross your fingers.

Audio 19.2

We mustn't go into full production yet.
You have to come up with ideas for the new product.

Audio 20.1

As you know, we introduced the Stellar range of office furniture in January in response to falling sales of the Orion range. We're at the end of the year now, so let's look at how the two products have performed in the four quarters of this year …

The red bars represent Orion and the green ones Stellar. Overall, you can immediately see how, as we expected, Orion sales have declined throughout the year, while Stellar sales have steadily increased.

Looking at Orion unit sales in more detail, they started quite brightly at the beginning of the year, but then fell to 34,000 in the second quarter, remained steady at 34 in Q3 before hitting a historic low of 18,000 at the end of the year.

Stellar, on the other hand, began with 16,000 units, but rose to 35,000 in Q2, then went up again by 10,000 to 45,000 in Q3. But the most striking feature is how Stellar has done in the last quarter of this year. Thanks to a gigantic effort by the team, we've done the impossible: sales have reached 51,000 in December. This is the best performance by any of our products in its first year.

Audio 20.2

unlikely, unlucky, unnecessary, unsuccessful
impatient, impolite
inefficient, informal
disadvantage, disagree
illegal, illogical
irregular, irrelevant

Audio 21.1

Interviewer: What kind of direct sales do you make, Henry?

Henry: In the past, we sold most of our products through our retail outlets. We have four shops in the south of England. Fifteen years ago, maybe 25% of our sales were mail-order sales. But with the internet and the popularity of our website, I would say that 60% of our business is now online. We have a few sales reps who demonstrate how our products perform in different conditions, and they go to shows around the world – not only in Europe, but also in Shanghai, Sydney and Miami.

Interviewer: How about indirect sales?

Henry: Oh yes, they're important, too. We currently sell to two large European sports retailers.

Interviewer: What is the process involved in selling to them?

Henry: Well, I can tell you how we started. Two years ago, one of our sales managers was lucky enough to meet one of their buyers at a boat show and arranged to make a presentation to them. This went well, and we followed up with much more detailed negotiations. They wanted to know everything about us, and eventually we got a contract with them.

Interviewer: What effect did this have on your business?

Henry: It was very significant. They buy in bulk, so we had to be careful about negotiating prices. The sales volumes went up, of course, so we had to be very careful to have the right amount of production and maintain the right levels of goods in stock.

Interviewer: Do you offer them sales discounts?

Henry: No, we don't offer them discounts, they demand them! There's a difference!

Interviewer: Ah.

Audio 21.2

We sell online, at boat shows, through agents and in our shops.

Audio 22.1

Manager: As you can see from the data here, there's been a marked improvement in our sales figures since launching Beach Accessories, and as I said in my e-mail, I intend to set the target at $100,000 for the next 12 months. Your area is the North Pacific, and I'll need you to make a sales forecast for the coming year.

Seller: Sure! I've looked at this already. Orders will probably be slow at the beginning of the year, so I guess sales will reach around $40,000 in the first quarter. Then, as the weather gets warmer, we'll get busier, and I expect them to pick up to about $80,000 in June.

Manager: And for the second half of the year?

Seller: The following few months are the busiest time of year for us, so I reckon we could sell another $100,000.

Manager: What about the last quarter?

Seller: Sales will slow down, of course, but we should still sell around $20,000.

Manager: That means you think you'll exceed targets.

Seller: We hope so, yes.

Manager: Great if you can do it! Can you send me those figures?

Seller: Yes, I'll e-mail them to you now.

Audio 22.2

1 in sales – an increase in sales – We've seen an increase in sales.
2 in July – to pick up in July – Sales are expected to pick up in July.
3 at the end of the year – performed well at the end of the year – The product performed well at the end of the year.
4 in the first quarter – were down 2% in the first quarter – Like-for-like sales were down 2% in the first quarter.
5 this year – 150,000 units this year – We're aiming to sell 150,000 units this year.

Audio 23.1

Woman: What are the main elements of the marketing mix at Manchester United?

Ben: First of all, the most important thing is that Manchester United provides an excellent football team that plays and wins in an exciting way. Their history includes some of the world's greatest and most recognisable players, such as David Beckham and Cristiano Ronaldo. However, there are other parts of the product, including merchandising – such as the sale of shirts – and a range of memorabilia, books and programmes. These are available to customers everywhere, as they are promoted and sold on the club's websites and in stores around the world. The product also relates to television rights.

Manchester United is a global brand. The club has a range of joint promotional activities, for example with our shirt sponsor Chevrolet. Promotion and revenue is also increased with a huge range of 'commerical partners', like DHL, Aeroflot and even Casillero del Diablo, which is the official wine of Manchester United. The club has positioned itself at the premier end of the market and charges premium prices, as you can see from the high cost of a season ticket to watch home league games. This is at Old Trafford – one of the biggest, most modern stadiums, with excellent facilities.

Audio 24.1

Interviewer: Vicky, how important is social networking in your job?

Vicky: Well, I work in marketing, and using social networks like Facebook and Twitter is essential. This is because I need to get news and information – about new products, promotions, etc. – out to a huge customer base. Five years ago, we used to send letters and leaflets out to hundreds of customers, which was time-consuming and expensive. But now customers have instant information at their fingertips … and, of course, it saves money with postage.

Interviewer: So you've managed to improve customer communication a lot?

Vicky: Yes, definitely – including keeping a live blog, which is updated throughout the day. Also, we can get immediate feedback from customers – they can contact us if they're happy with something, with any suggestions and of course if they have any problems.

Interviewer: I guess, then, that it's a great way to do market research at very little cost!

Vicky: Exactly!

Interviewer: Do you use social networking for anything else?

Vicky: Yes, it's also an important part of my job.

Interviewer: How do you mean?

Vicky: Well, through social networking, I can easily keep in touch with my contacts in the industry. I can find out what's happening – new products or promotions from our competitors – and keep up to date with the latest trends.

Interviewer: Vicky, thank you.

Audio 24.2

We used to send letters and leaflets.
We used to produce paper catalogues.
Requesting confirmation used to be very slow.

Audio 25.1

Mark: Can you just explain again, Carmel, what the problem is exactly?

Carmel: Certainly, it's quite simple. The Hobsons account was $280,000 in the red at the end of April, but only $270,000 in debt at the end of May.

Mark: And Hobsons made no payment in April, you're sure of that?

Carmel: Absolutely.

Naresh: Are you saying that somebody here has been falsifying the accounts?

Carmel: I can't see any other explanation.

Naresh: Have you spoken to Hobsons yet?

Carmel: No, not yet.

Mark: I don't think we should speak to Hobsons yet. We have to find out what happened here first.

Carmel: I agree entirely. There's no point in bringing them into it at this stage. First of all, we have to carry out an audit here.

Naresh: Yeah, I see what you mean, but it might be an idea to invite somebody from outside to do the audit.

Carmel: I can't agree with that – are you suggesting we aren't capable of carrying out our own internal audit or – even worse – that we aren't to be trusted?

Mark: No, nobody's saying that the Finance Department can't be trusted. First of all, we'll do an internal check, and if that doesn't turn up anything, we'll take it to the next stage.

Su: Could I just say something here? This isn't the first time this has happened, you know. I can remember when we had exactly the same problem, and we found out it was just a mistake, somebody had written …

Audio 25.2

1 I'd like to welcome Mr Kaya to Turkey.
2 It seems to me that there are two problems.
3 It's very important that you have a clear idea about this.
4 It's as fast as lightning.
5 There are three reasons for this.
6 Could I just make a point about that?
7 How about trying another supplier?

Audio 27.1

James: Right, so let's try to get a clearer picture of what's going on here with a SWOT analysis.

Emma: A what analysis?

James: A SWOT analysis – we're going to look at the business in terms of its strengths, weaknesses, opportunities and threats. Here, look.

Emma: OK, if you say so.

James: Now, what are our strong points?

Emma: Well, our position – we're right in the centre of the city here.

James: Yes, and we've got a good customer base, lots of regular customers.

Emma: Mm-hm. Also, our food. I mean, nobody else round here offers our kind of lunchtime service, our fast food …

James: OK. Um, weaknesses. Well, it's very small, isn't it? Some customers can sit outside, but we've only got four tables inside. I know that's lost us some customers.

Emma: Yes. And the kitchen's too small as well – it's impossible to work in there sometimes.

James: Yeah, and we've got no licence to sell alcohol …

Emma: No, and I don't think we'll be able to get one.

James: Hm. Opportunities now. Well, the new office development being built opposite us has got to be an opportunity. I mean, there are going to be hundreds of new office workers in there next year.

Emma: Yeah, absolutely, and with that I'd say we should definitely think about starting a website so they could order food and drinks at their desks.

James: Mm, good idea. What about threats? Of course, there's that new restaurant down the road, what, about a hundred metres from here?

Emma: Yeah, I'm a bit worried about that. I don't think our customers would go there – they haven't got the time – but you never know.

James: Yes, and another threat is the rent. They're going to put it up again this year, I'm sure, and that's going to really affect …

Audio 27.2

1 What was the name of the restaurant?
2 If I were you, I'd look for a new office.
3 We're going to look at the strengths, weaknesses, opportunities and threats.
4 Some customers can sit outside.
5 We should definitely think about starting a website so customers could order food and drinks at their desks.

Audio 28.1

1 **Man 1:** We've looked at your performance over the last year.

   Man 2: Yes.

   Man 1: We've been really impressed with your dedication, and you've always hit your sales targets. So we'd like to offer you a 5% pay increase.

   Man 2: Thank you, but I was really hoping for a higher figure – like 10%.

   Man 1: Hmmm.

Audio 28.2

2 **Man:** You say that you've been in your new role for eight months now, but you still don't know all aspects of the IT system.

   Woman: That's right. I feel I've been thrown in at the deep end without any sort of preparation or guidance.

   Man: I see. How about if we put you on a systems refresher course and get your team leader to follow up with specific training on different modules?

   Woman: That sounds great.

Audio 28.3

3 **Man 1:** I'm afraid that the quality of your work hasn't been good enough. We really expect much more from our employees.

   Man 2: Well, I think that if I was appointed as the new team leader, I'd work much harder.

   Man 1: I'm sorry, but you need to *earn* a position like that, with more responsibility, and so far we don't think this would be justified.

Audio 28.4

answering, biscuit, business, calm, debt, guest, guide, high, hour, island, sign, vehicle, Wednesday, whole, would

Audio 29.1

1 These figures show earnings for the first six months.
2 Do I have to sign here?
3 Go to our homepage to find the link to the accounts.
4 I wanted to ask you about the overheads.
5 See you again soon.

Audio 29.2

1 Revenue, or turnover, is at the top of the P&L.
2 Labour and materials are direct costs.
3 The gross profit is calculated after direct costs have been deducted.
4 After the gross profit, the next line of profit before tax and interest is the operating profit.
5 Rent and the internet are examples of indirect costs.
6 The bottom line is the net profit, which shows earnings after tax and interest paid.
7 The return is the ratio of money gained or lost on an investment in relation to the amount of money invested.

Audio 30.1

Chair: Good afternoon, everybody. Does everyone have a copy of the agenda? Good. Now, the reason we're here today is to decide on three issues in particular. I'd like to aim for a five o'clock finish, so let's get started. Item one on the agenda, and the most urgent matter, is the number of calls that we're receiving from customers about the steering-wheel lock.

William: Could I just say that we still haven't decided what we're going to do about the pricing review.

Chair: Yes, William, true, but I suggest we deal with that at next week's meeting. Now, as I was saying … the calls that we're receiving from customers about the steering-wheel lock. First, I'd like to hear how you're currently dealing with the problem. Can we go round the table on this? Jasmine?

Jasmine: We've also got a problem with the fan heater in the PX2 model – when you switch it on to three, sometimes it …

Chair: Can we just discuss the steering-wheel lock for now, please, Jasmine?

Jasmine: Oh, OK, sure. Well, the problem with that is that when the driver turns the key in the lock, 99 times out of a hundred, the lock will automatically …

* * * * *

Chair: Let's move on to the next point on the agenda: the problem with an important customer of ours, Western Garages, and the repeated complaints we're getting from them. We need to identify exactly why these complaints keep coming in and decide on how to respond. Are they really all different complaints, or is there another reason behind this that we haven't identified …

* * * * *

Has anyone got anything to add? No? Right, well, now we come to our third and final point, the PX3 catalogue. As you know, the catalogue states that the PX3 has a warranty of three years. However, some customers have been claiming that …

* * * * *

So, we've nearly finished for today, but first we need to settle the action plan. William, you're going to organise a meeting with Western. Lucy, it's your job to write up and distribute the procedure for responding to the steering-lock problem; and Simona, I want you to check our legal position regarding the catalogue and the PX3 model and get back to me by tomorrow afternoon. OK?

Audio 31.1

Interviewer: Amir, can you tell us about how your company recruits new people? What's the recruitment process?

Amir: Well, I work out of our Kuala Lumpur office, and it's my job to make sure that we employ the most suitable people for the available positions in the Risk Assessment sector. We follow quite a strict procedure. First, we advertise the job through recruitment agencies and online on our company website.

Interviewer: I see. And what's the next step in the process?

Amir: Then we look through the CVs that we receive and decide which candidates have suitable skills, as well as the necessary experience and knowledge for the position. Then we group the applicants into those who meet the minimum job requirements and those who don't … creating a shortlist of applicants. And the next step is a telephone interview.

Interviewer: And then you hire them?

Amir: No! It's a bit more complicated than that. If they pass this selection process, we ask for three references.

Interviewer: References?

Amir: Yes, three people who support the applicant. Normally, your current boss or supervisor and your previous one. And the final one is a personal reference, usually a friend, relative or a professional – for example, a lawyer, teacher, accountant – who can vouch for you. We then contact these people and ask them to send a letter of reference directly to us.

Interviewer: What happens then?

Amir: Basically, there are two more interviews.

Interviewer: Two more?

Amir: Yes, there's an onsite interview with my colleagues from the HR department and then a final interview with at least two department managers.

Interviewer: And then?

Amir: If they're successful in that last interview, then we can negotiate the terms for their contract. This involves arranging the salary, company benefits (like private pension, healthcare, car, etc.) and holiday entitlements.

Interviewer: Is that the final step?

Amir: Yes. Then finally the candidate is taken on.

Audio 31.2

You like working in teams?
He's finished already?
Your CV is up to date?
You're leaving now?
This is the last interview?

Audio 32.1

Mette: I believe that companies in the future are likely to want more and more data about their customers in order to make decisions on strategy. This might become an even more controversial privacy issue than it is today. Why will this happen? Because the digital revolution of the last 25 years has meant that global economies are becoming increasingly linked with each other, and business, industries and governments will soon have to co-operate much more with each other on an international scale than they've ever done before. The markets – both individuals and businesses – are very hungry for faster, bigger, better communication, so I'm sure this interconnection will continue and grow.

Another global trend we're witnessing today which will affect us much more in the future is the changing population. We have a growing global population which is bound to continue to grow in the future, but at the same time, in many countries, we also have a shrinking workforce due to people getting older. Some countries already have more people leaving employment than entering it – in Japan, for example – and we're going to see more of this in the future. On the other hand, this can be an opportunity for other countries with a young workforce, such as India and Brazil. India, in fact, has one-third of the population under 15 years of age; they might be a huge asset to their economy if they're properly trained.

So, this brings us to another major trend affecting the future of global business, and that's the rise of the so-called BRICS countries: Brazil, Russia, India, China and South Africa. These will continue to be the main engines of the world's economic growth. In the last ten years, …

Audio 32.2

1 I won't go.
2 They want to come.
3 You won't do it.
4 We want to pay the bill.

Audio 32.3

1 I won't go.   I want to go.
2 They won't come.   They want to come.
3 You won't do it.   You want to do it.
4 We won't pay the bill.   We want to pay the bill.

Audio 32.4

1 I'll go.
2 We'll help you.
3 You work hard.
4 They'll play golf.

Audio 32.5

1 I go.   I'll go.
2 We help you.   We'll help you.
3 You work hard.   You'll work hard.
4 They play golf.   They'll play golf.

Audio 33.1

Kate: Right – the first thing we have to do is identify risks.
Phil: OK, but before that, I think we should look at what the key areas of the business are.
Kate: All right … well, the people – us and the staff.
Phil: And the guests, of course!
Kate: Yes, then the building – the hotel itself.
Phil: And the essential services like water, electricity …
Kate: Yes, and the computer system.
Phil: OK, well, what could go wrong? Let's make a list.
Kate: Well, we know that flooding is a real risk round here.
Phil: Yes, and there's fire.
Kate: Mm. Yes – also, problems with the food – food poisoning.
Phil: OK, and no guests. I mean, if people stopped coming to the hotel for a few months, what would we do? We couldn't pay the bills.
Kate: True. What else? A breakdown in the services. If we had a power cut, for example.
Phil: Yep, and noise. You know there are plans to build an office block across the road …
Kate: Yes, that's going to be noisy. And crime, by one of the staff or a guest or an outsider.
Phil: Vandalism. We've already had some of that.
Kate: Yes, that's included in crime …
Phil: Murder.
Kate: That's not very likely.
Phil: Nuclear attack?
Kate: That's enough, Phil! … Now, contingency plans. What would we do if there was a flood?
Phil: Yeah, that's a real risk. You know what happened near here last year.
Kate: Well, of course the first priority is the safety of the people, so we'd need to evacuate the hotel and move them to a safe place.
Phil: Yes, we haven't thought about that before, have we?
Kate: How about moving them up to Samantha's hotel, The Grange? That's much higher than us.
Phil: Yes, that's an idea. We'll have to speak to her. I'll call her this evening and arrange to meet.
Kate: Then there's the building. We really ought to take some precautions, think about what we can do now in case of a flood.
Phil: Yes, what should we do?
Kate: Mm, it's tricky. Maybe we should speak to the local authorities – the council or the Environment Agency.
Phil: OK, let's do that.
Kate: Now, what if we had a power cut?

Audio 34.1

Woman: Why did you move your production centre?
Enrico: With the increasingly competitive market and the economic downturn, it was necessary to look at ways to lower our production costs.
Woman: Which location did you choose?
Enrico: We looked at various places, but decided to use a location near to Italy: Tunisia.
Woman: Why did you choose Tunisia?
Enrico: Well, construction costs are a lot cheaper than in Italy, and we were able to build a brand-new manufacturing plant with the latest and most efficient technology. Then there's the huge available workforce, and we don't have to pay the high labour costs – both wages and taxes – of Europe. And because it's nearer Italy, it's cheap and efficient to visit and manage.
Woman: So will you move all your business to Tunisia in the future?
Enrico: Definitely not. We're still very much an Italian company. All our research and development is still based in Italy. Also, for non-standard or unusual product requests and priority orders, our original factory is still available … at a higher cost of course!

Audio 34.2

consume, educated, focus, fruit, include, juice, June, manufacture, produce, rule, supply, support, Tunisia, usual

Audio 35.1

In 2013, Australia's GDP was increasing at 3.8%, following more than 20 years of continuous economic growth averaging 3.5% a year. The annual rate of inflation is around 2 to 3 per cent, and unemployment in 2013 was at 5.8%.

In the same year, the proportion of those with wealth above 100,000 US dollars was the highest of any country, eight times the world average, while 12% of the population were living below the poverty line.

In the primary sector, Australia is rich in commodities, particularly mineral resources such as coal, iron, copper, gold and natural gas. Demand for these from Asia – and especially China – has grown rapidly. Despite environmental concerns, Australia is the world's leading coal exporter, and it provides about 85% of Australia's own electricity production.

The country also has a rich and varied agriculture of crops and livestock, exporting more than half of its output.

In the secondary sector, the high value of the currency, the Australian dollar, has damaged manufacturing, which is now half what it was in the 1960s.

The services sector, on the other hand, accounts for the largest part of the Australian economy, in particular finance and tourism. Some of its largest companies include the mining corporations BHP Billiton and Rio Tinto, as well as the National Australia Bank.

Australia has free-trade agreements with Chile, Malaysia, New Zealand, Singapore, Thailand and the US, and is negotiating agreements with China, India, Indonesia, Japan and the Republic of Korea.

Audio 35.2

an export, to export, an increase, to increase, an import, to import

Audio 35.3

commodities, economy, employment, government, industry, percentage

Audio 36.1

There are several quite easy ways companies can become more environmentally friendly. What a lot of businesses often don't realise is that this often brings several other benefits, such as cutting costs and improving your reputation. One of the biggest costs for companies can be heating in the winter and cooling in the summer. So first of all, make sure you have maximum and minimum temperatures you can control, and don't waste money heating and cooling rooms that aren't used. Next, install occupancy sensors. This means lights automatically switch on or off depending on whether anybody's there. These can be used in toilets, for example. Then, don't waste paper. Research has shown that there are five copies of the average document on computers, so there's no need to print another one. Some people print copies of e-mails. What's the point? And if you have to print, then print double-sided. Next, try to buy office supplies, like paper, locally. If you buy from out of town, you're using transport, which damages the environment. Then there's car sharing, or car pooling. Encourage your employees to share their cars instead of each person travelling in their own car. You can do this by offering these people special benefits, like their own parking spaces.

Audio 37.1

Before you arrive at a Lush shop, you can smell it. I mean, there's a really strong smell of spices, fruit and flowers. Some people find it too much, but you can't ignore it. When you get into the shop, you can see why the smell is so strong, because there's very little packaging. Lots and lots of soaps are on tables and shelves like pieces of cheese. In fact, when I was in there, the look, feel and smell of some of the goods made me think 'Am I supposed to put this on my face or eat it?' I found the atmosphere warmer and more welcoming than other shops, and the service is excellent. I don't know any other stores or products like these.

There are other reasons why Lush is so different from its competitors. It does very little advertising. The shop itself is a kind of advert, and they have a catalogue which they invite you to take when you make a purchase. But they've built most of their reputation from word of mouth – customers telling other people.

And what about the prices? Well, they're pretty high, but I think that's worked too, because the customers keep coming back, a clear message that the product quality is good too.

Mr and Mrs Constantine understood the competition and the fact that customers wanted something more, something different.

Audio 37.2

1 Their price is the same as ours.
2 The atmosphere is warmer and more welcoming than other shops.
3 Lush is very different from its competitors.
4 Our costs aren't as high as theirs.
5 Their market share is bigger than ours.

Audio 38.1

1 The people in the meeting all seemed to have the same idea. I found it difficult to understand what their individual opinions of the deal were.
2 He asked us to send him our catalogue as soon as we have some new products. I suppose that means he's not interested in buying now.
3 I don't understand why there's this delay. It clearly states in our terms and conditions that a discount is only offered on purchases over 500.
4 **A:** Would you like some more cake?
  B: No, thanks.
5 **A:** Katherine, this is Thomas Jackson, Head of Marketing for North America.
  B: Hi, Katherine, just call me Tom.

Audio 39.1

Euan: My name is Euan Van Reep. I ran a virtual team for six months as the project manager of a website. I'm located in The Hague, Netherlands. The website was designed in Seoul, in the Republic of Korea. The software was developed in Brisbane, Australia. Most of the communication was via instant messaging and also through data conferencing. I only had one face-to-face meeting with the team leader for the technology development last December.

Danny: I'm Danny Lee and I've been Head of Product Forecasting in South-East Asia for two years. To do this, I need to understand what the market needs and what the factory can do. Therefore I have to keep in touch with the head office in Singapore, the staff in Kuala Lumpur, Malaysia, and the factory in Jakarta, Indonesia. E-mail and phone calls are my main tools when working. I also have discussions via video-conference systems and make a lot of business trips around South-East Asia.

Audio 40.1

Announcer: Now here's Peter Cox with today's financial news.
Peter: Yes, thank you, Anne. Well, it's generally been a very poor day for the markets, and the one-hundred index has closed down 2.4 points at 4016. PB Oil was today's biggest loser – down 10%, from 1,500 cents to 1,350. This had a negative effect on the rest of the market. PH Pharmaceuticals also fell, from 1,000 cents to 800 cents. Tower Insurance didn't go down so heavily, but still lost 10 cents to finish at 240 cents. Phonecom, meanwhile, has remained steady at 150 cents a share. As sometimes happens in this kind of situation, things were better for investors in smaller companies; for example Bridge Automobiles' stocks doubled from 50 cents to 100 cents with news of the launch of their gas-engined car, Fulchester Football Club's value increased from 100 to 150 cents, and Palace Leisure continues strongly – up 30 to 180 cents.

Audio 40.2

Announcer: Now it's over to Peter Cox for today's market news. Peter?
Peter: Yes, thanks, Anne. Well, a lively day today, with the stock market eventually closing up half a point at 3,090. Amongst today's biggest losers were two companies who've had real problems with the safety of their products recently. Following a very negative Medical Council report on BexBio's flu treatment, and the resignation of their chairman, shares in the company were trading at 500 cents this afternoon, while Bridge Automobiles' problems with the safety of their gas-engined cars continued – they lost 60 cents to finish the day at 40. Mediamix's involvement in the Sanderson accounting scandal cut their price sharply to 150 cents, and some disastrous decisions at Guilders, with one trader in particular losing them more than one billion euros, has reduced the investment company's share value to 300 cents. Fulchester FC have not won a single match so far this season, and this form is reflected in their share price, down to 100 cents.
And today's winners? Well, fears of war have caused the gold price to rise to 500 cents a gram, and Blue K Mines reached 100 cents at the close today. For the same reason, PB Oil made good gains and finished at 1,500 cents.
And finally, some sweet music for those supporters of Rockit Recording – after their phenomenal success in the worlds of music and film, they now plan to move into television production. My advice is to buy, even at today's closing price of 210 cents.

Answer key

Unit 1

2 one year in Hamburg (not Paris)
BSc in Business Studies (not Computer Studies)
cell number 09435 683927 (not 683957)

3 I'm currently working as …
I've only been working for [PTK] since [2011].
I have experience in …
I have a Bachelor's degree in … from …

4 *Suggested answers*
Where were you born?
What professional qualifications do you have?
What's your current job title?
Where did you work before?
How long have you been working for your current employer?
What are you working on at the moment?
Do you have any experience in …?
Have you done any training courses?
What do you like to do in your spare time?

Pronunciation 1
2 He's qualified‿as‿an‿engineer.
3 She's got‿a degree in‿economics.
4 He resigned‿on Friday.
5 I'm currently working‿as‿a flight‿attendant.
6 She went‿out‿at‿eight.
7 He sent‿in his CV to the company.

Unit 2

2 1 Executive Assistant   2 Organisation Analyst
3 Factory Manager

3 The main thing I (aim to) do is …
I have to (help / study / report to / set up / follow up) …
Another important part of my job is …
It's my job to …
I'm (also) responsible for …
I'm in charge of …
The main purpose of my job is to …

Pronunciation 1
1 /pɜːsənˈel/   2 /ˈpɜːpəs/   3 /ɔːlˈðəʊ/   4 /ˈkɒliːgz/
5 /ˈænəlaɪz/   6 /əˈnæləsɪs/   7 /suːt/   8 /emplɔɪˈiːz/

4 1 prepare   2 co-ordinating   3 improve   4 answering
5 liaise   6 seeing

Unit 3

2 1 Milan   2 car   3 Gatwick Station   4 return to Gatwick
5 taxi   6 £70   7 hotel   8 hotel full – stay

3 1 I got stuck in traffic   2 we took off an hour late   3 got on
the wrong train   4 take a cab   5 received any confirmation
of the booking (and the hotel was full)

4 1 pick [me] up   2 took off   3 set off   4 held up
5 checked in   6 dropped [me] off

Pronunciation 1
arrived: 2   asked: 1   decided: 3   delayed: 2   landed: 2
looked: 1   missed: 1   parked: 1   realised: 3   received: 2
rushed: 1   seemed: 1   stayed: 1   threatened: 2
visited: 3   waited: 2   wanted: 2   worked: 1

Pronunciation 2

/t/	/d/	/ɪd/
asked, looked, missed, parked, rushed, worked	arrived, delayed, realised, received, seemed, stayed, threatened	decided, landed, visited, waited, wanted

6 Where did you go? Why?
Can you describe your journey?
How long did it take to get there?
Were you delayed? / Was the flight delayed? Why?
What time did you/it arrive?
Where did you stay?
Who did you meet?
What did you talk about / discuss?
What did you do there?
Did you visit anywhere in particular?
What was the food like?
What was the weather like?
Were there / Did you have any problems? What?
How much did you spend?
Who paid (for the trip)?
Would you like to go there again?

Unit 4

2 1 a   2 a   3 a   4 c   5 c   6 b

3 1 bill   2 off   3 rent   4 by credit/debit card   5 for   6 cash

4 1 lend   2 earn   3 borrow   4 own   5 borrow   6 afford

Unit 5

3 It is a technique that involves starting with the end result of a
problem and asking a series of *why* questions until you get to
the root of the problem.

4 1 Because their prices have increased.
2 Because of their increased costs.
3 Because they only buy their supplies from the USA, and the
dollar–euro exchange rate is very poor now.
4 Because they get good-quality components on time.
5 Because they haven't had time to do the research.

Pronunciation 1
1 don't   2 I'd   3 They've   4 didn't   5 shouldn't   6 I'll

Unit 6

1

Vegetable	Fruit
aubergine, leek, potato, cucumber, radish, rocket, artichokes, broccoli, peas, onions, mushrooms, beans, lettuce	figs, tomato(es), olive, apple, cranberry, lemon, blackcurrants, apricot, blackberry, raspberry, melon, pineapple, grapes, kiwi, grapefruit, rhubarb

Meat	Fish/Seafood	Other
Parma ham, pork, beef, chicken, liver, duck	mackerel, sea bass, cod, prawns	cheese, walnuts, blue cheese, butter, garlic, dumplings, chickpea, (egg-fried) rice, parmesan, chocolate, cream , ice cream

2 **Starters:** Baked aubergine, Mackerel
Main course: Sea bass, Stir-fried beef
Desserts: –
Drinks: half bottle of dry white wine (house white – Pinot
Grigio), half a litre of still water

3 Vegetarians

Pronunciation 1
/ð/ voiced: although, clothes, other, that, the, then, there,
together
/θ/ unvoiced: both, healthy, mouth, something, teeth, thank,
thing, think

Unit 7

1 1 C 2 B 3 A 4 B, C 5 C

3 1 GT Zurich → JT Zurich
from the Marriott Hotel to the Rex → from the Rex Hotel to the Marriott

2 Pecnam → Becman
Friday 28th → Friday 21st
SP46DT → FP56DT
missing a drill → missing two drills
01342 499864 → 01342 599864

3 £100 → £1,000
portmeck@freestyle.co.uk → portmech@freestyle.co.uk

Unit 8

2 1 F (The purpose of the talk is to explain the customer-complaints procedure however the complaint is received.)
2 T
3 T
4 F (They work in groups.)

3 The purpose of this talk this morning is to …
If you have any questions, please feel free to interrupt.
As you can see from this diagram, …
We've seen … now let's move on to …
I must emphasise that …
I hope that's given you a clear picture of …
Are there any more questions?

Pronunciation 1

1 These are not <u>suggestions</u> for steps, they are the <u>only</u> <u>way</u> you are allowed to answer.
2 I don't want to lower <u>some</u> of our prices, I want to lower <u>all</u> of our prices.
3 As you can see from the graph, sales didn't go <u>down</u> in June, they went <u>up</u>.

Pronunciation 3

1 No, he hasn't gone to <u>Detroit</u>, he's gone to <u>Chicago</u>.
2 I called on Wednesday <u>and</u> Thursday.
3 I <u>have</u> finished the report.

Unit 9

1 *Suggested answers*
1 Good advice. This can affect the preparation of your presentation. How many people will be there? Who will be there? What interests them? What do they know already?
2 It depends. If you have data to present, PowerPoint can be a useful tool. But if you're going to use slides, don't just read them out word for word, and make sure all the audience can see them.
3 Good advice. The more you can engage the audience, the better.
4 Good advice. Nobody's going to mind if you go a few minutes over your time, but any more can cause problems for the audience and other speakers. Plan carefully to finish on time.
5 It depends. On the whole, it can be a good idea to vary your media, but not too much. If you have a good reason for choosing a chart, a photograph or a video, then use it. Using lots of colour can make an impact and make your presentation memorable, but be careful not to overwhelm your audience.
6 Good advice. It's a good idea to make eye contact with people across the audience, but not for too long with the same person
7 Bad advice. It's advisable to have some water available to sip when your mouth gets dry, but don't drink too much (you may end up needing to go to the toilet in the middle of your presentation!) and don't drink iced water, as it can constrict your throat.
8 Bad advice. Just be as natural as you can.
9 It depends. It's not a good idea to start your presentation with an apology for being nervous or anything else, as you're focusing on a negative before you begin! But acknowledge a mistake if you make one.

3 c

4 I'm sure you all agree that …
We must do something about …
Let's look at this in more detail.
In particular …
What's the point?

It makes sense to …
I strongly suggest …

Pronunciation 2

Let's look at this <u>question</u> of <u>company</u> <u>assets</u> in more <u>detail</u>, in <u>particular</u> <u>machinery</u>. Our <u>yard</u> here is <u>full</u> of <u>machinery</u> that we're <u>repairing</u> – and <u>yes</u>, I'll admit that we <u>are</u> <u>good</u> at <u>repairing</u> <u>broken</u> and <u>old</u> <u>machinery</u> – but our <u>core</u> <u>business</u> is <u>construction</u>, not <u>machinery</u> <u>maintenance</u> – or it <u>should</u> be! If we look at one of our <u>competitors</u> – Watson's, for example – in <u>November</u> last year, we had <u>140</u> <u>items</u> of <u>machinery</u> on <u>site</u>, whereas <u>they</u> had just <u>30</u>! Yes, <u>30</u>! We had more or less the <u>same number</u> of <u>contracts</u>, but <u>compared</u> with <u>them</u>, we had nearly <u>five times</u> the <u>amount</u> of <u>machinery</u>. <u>Why</u>? What's the <u>point</u>? It's just a <u>cost</u>!

Unit 10

1 *Suggested answers*
Woman 2 is not paying attention to what woman 1 is saying.
Man 2 is giving a one-word answer to man 1's question.
Both of the above would make the speaker appear rude and uninterested.
Man 3 is worrying unnecessarily about how he expresses himself, rather than concentrating on communicating. It is usually better to keep a conversation going, even if you make a few mistakes.

2 1 g 2 b 3 e 4 c 5 f 6 a 7 d 8 h

Unit 11

1 1 c 2 a 3 e 4 b 5 d
2 1 T 2 T 3 T 4 T
3 I'm calling about …
Sorry, I don't follow you.
Could you speak a bit more slowly, please?
Sorry, what do you mean?
I see.
Uh-huh.
So what you're saying is …
OK.
I'll need to check and get back to you.
Could you confirm […] by e-mail, please?

Unit 12

1 She should start by 15th November this year.
4

Not urgent Important	Urgent Important
2, 5, 7	4, 6, 8
Not urgent Unimportant	Urgent Unimportant
3, 10	1, 9

Pronunciation 1

/aɪ/ **time**	/eɪ/ **main**	/əʊ/ **go**	/eə/ **fair**	/ɪə/ **near**
decide	campaign	know	dare	beer
price	delay	most	prepare	dear
priority	straight	slow	share	gear
right	waste	so	their	here

5 1 waste/spend 2 on 3 straight/right 4 takes/took
5 lead 6 by/on

Unit 13

1 *Suggested answers*
1 You must be on time for your interview; lateness gives a very poor impression.
2 Before the interview, you should demonstrate your enthusiasm by finding out as much as you can about the organisation you're hoping to work with.
3 Employers are mainly interested in what you can offer the business, not your need for a job.
4 You must always switch off your mobile phone before you go into an interview. You do not want any interruptions, and you certainly don't want to give the impression that you have other, more important things to do.
5 You should never criticise your previous boss – your new employers will suspect you'd do the same about them in the future.

6 This is not the best question to start with. You should wait till the interviewer brings it up if possible, or at least wait until the end of the interview.

7 Be honest! Interviewers will wonder what you're trying to hide.

8 You should show interest and evidence of preparation for the interview, so think of something to ask.

2 Ms Budka got the job, because she gave a short but succinct description of herself in relation to her application. She was well prepared for the question asking what she knew about the bank.

Mr Edmondson made several mistakes: he shouldn't have complimented the interviewer on her appearance; he didn't know much about the bank; he shouldn't have interrupted the line of questioning to ask whether he would have his own office.

3 What can you tell us about yourself?
Tell us what you know about our bank.
What do you know about our bank?
Can you tell us who else you've applied to?

4 1 creative   2 determined/motivated/focused
3 loyal/reliable   4 sociable   5 adaptable   6 practical

6 1 assisted   2 worked on / set up   3 managed/supervised/led   4 carried out   5 built / organised / set up
6 worked on / planned

7 Question B is an indirect question. The interrogative form of the main verb changes to the affirmative form.

8 *Possible answers*
Could you tell us where you worked before your current job?
Tell me when you left school.
I'd like to know why you want to work for us.
Could you tell us what you know about our company?
Tell me why you left your last job.
We'd like to know how much you expect to be paid.

Unit 14

2 1 reports   2 HR   3 HR Directors   4 Purchasing Department
5 journalists   6 politicians

3 1 T   2 F (They discuss proposals and progress.)
3 T   4 T   5 T

Pronunciation 1
There are 14 schwa sounds.
1 I talked to Jack about the date.
2 They asked us for more money.
3 His boss shouted at him when he made a mistake.
4 I reminded her of the appointment.
5 They blamed me for the mistake.
6 We warned them about the danger.

Unit 15

2 1 d   2 c   3 a   4 b

3 1 F (He says they can be flat or hierarchical.)   2 T
3 F (Functional structures group people according to their jobs.)   4 T

4 (from top down) Marketing Director, Group Product Manager, Senior Brand Manager, Brand Manager, Assistant Brand Manager

Pronunciation 1
charge, hierarchy, marketing (/ɑː/)
confirm, early, virtual, work, world (/ɜː/)
law, reports, resources, walk (/ɔː/)
parent, shares (/eə/)

6 1 No, it's a private limited company.
2 Yes, it's a subsidiary of Jonson's.
3 In the US
4 In Amsterdam, the Netherlands
5 It has a hierarchical structure.
6 The President
7 The Marketing Director

Unit 16

1 2 and 4

3 1 mayonnaise   2 an investment account   3 software
4 a 3D camcorder

4 1 The product needs to be a little creamier for the **German** market.
2 Interest is paid either monthly or yearly, **before** tax.
3 You also get free online **assistance** if you have problems.
4 The **retail** price is very reasonable, just $950.

5 1 memory stick: c, f, h, j
2 bicycle tyres: b, e, g, k
3 holidays for retired people: a, d, i, l

Unit 17

1 1 c   2 f   3 b   4 a   5 d   6 e

2 a 4   b 3   c 2   d 5   e 6   f 1

Pronunciation 1
You usually pause after the sequencing words or phrases.

3 It shows the process involved in a car-insurance claim.

4 a If the claim is accepted, the customer is paid by the insurance company.
b The claim is evaluated by the insurance company.
c A claim is made by the customer.
d If the claim is rejected by the insurers, they refuse to pay the customer.
e The paid claim is filed by the insurers for future reference.
f The accident is reported by the customer to the insurance company.

5 See audio script 17.2.

Unit 18

2 1 Alex works for Fiat and Kaito works for Nissan.
2 They've both worked on traditional high-performance engines.
3 In the UK.
4 Because they may be recruiting engineers.

3 1 So am I   2 Really, did you   3 Are they
4 Would you like to join me

4 *Short questions as follows:*
1 Are you?   2 Did you?   3 Can't she?   4 Were you?
5 Haven't you?   6 Does she?   7 Do you?   8 Didn't you?

5 *Phrases for agreement as follows:*
1 So am I.   2 So did I.   3 Neither can I.   4 So was I.
5 Neither have I.   6 So do I.   7 So do I.   8 Neither did I.

Pronunciation 2
See audio script 18.4.

Unit 19

3 clearly define the product 5
come up with ideas 2
develop it 6
do market research 1
evaluate ideas 3
invest in an idea 4
launch the product 9
make some samples 7
promote it in multiple channels 10
test it 8
underline its advantages and benefits 11

4 1 need to   2 have to   3 shouldn't   4 mustn't   5 should
6 've got to

Pronunciation 1
1 The letter 't'   2 /hæf/

5 *Suggested answers*
1 They should have tested it.
2 They didn't promote it enough.
3 They should have calculated the return on investment.
4 They didn't do enough market research.
5 They needed to clearly define the product.

Unit 20

1 1 a 2 c 3 d 4 b

2 **Comparative sales of *Orion* and *Stellar* office furniture ranges**

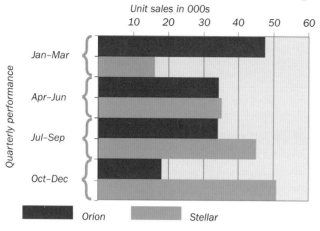

Pronunciation 1

un-	im-	in-
unlikely unlucky unnecessary unsuccessful	impatient impolite	inefficient informal

dis-	il-	ir-
disadvantage disagree	illegal illogical	irregular irrelevant

Unit 21

2 direct sales: retail outlets (four shops), mail-order sales (25% 15 years ago, now 60%), sales reps (boat shows)
indirect sales: two large European sports retailers

3 direct sales, retail outlet, sales rep, indirect sales, to buy in bulk, to negotiate prices, sales volume, goods in stock, sales discount

4 1 prospect 2 invoice 3 out 4 point 5 dealer 6 off
7 purchases 8 volume

Unit 22

2 July to September (the third quarter)

3 1 an increase 2 set 3 reach; $40,000 4 pick up
5 slow down

4 *Suggested answers*
  1 set a sales target / set a goal/objective
  2 Sales slowed down. / The product performed badly.
  3 exceed a sales target / The product performed well.
  4 make/create a sales forecast
  5 The product performed quite well overall.

5 1 e 2 b 3 a 4 d 5 f 6 c

Unit 23

3 1 merchandising 2 promoted 3 television rights 4 brand
5 promotional activities 6 premium prices

4 product: excellent, exciting team, merchandising, TV rights
price: premium prices
place: websites and stores
promotion: through sponsors and commercial partners
people: famous, recognisable players

5 1 c 2 e 3 d 4 b 5 a

Unit 24

3 get news and information out, information at your fingertips, improve customer communication, keep a live blog, immediate feedback, keep in touch with, keep up to date with

4 1 Five years ago, we used to send letters and **leaflets** out to customers.

2 Customer communication has **not** improved a lot.
3 We can get immediate feedback if **customers** are happy with something and if they have any problems.
4 **Social networking** is also an important part of my job.
5 Through social networking, I can keep in touch with my **contacts**.

5 1 e 2 c 3 b 4 d 5 a

Unit 25

3 Either someone has been falsifying the accounts, or a mistake has been made.

4 1 Are you saying 2 I agree entirely 3 I see what you mean
4 Could I just say something here

Pronunciation 1

  1 to; to 2 that 3 that; a; about 4 as; as 5 are; for
  6 a 7 about

Unit 26

1 right, well, so, er, actually, I mean

Unit 27

1 1 Opportunities 2 Weaknesses 3 Threats 4 Strengths

2

Strengths	Weaknesses
• The café is in the centre of the city. • Good, regular customer base. • No one else offers their kind of service and fast food.	• There is only space for four tables in the café. • Kitchen is too small. • No alcohol licence, and little possibility of getting one.
Opportunities	**Threats**
• A new large office development is being built opposite. • Start an online order service.	• Next month, a new restaurant is opening 100 metres away. • Owner of building is likely to put the rent up soon.

3 *Suggested answers*
  1 If I were you, I'd apply for permission to try to expand the space inside or outside.
  2 I suppose you could apply for a licence or put up a notice inviting guests to bring their own alcoholic drinks.
  3 Why don't you look at the possibilities of expanding the space available?
  4 Couldn't you differentiate your restaurant clearly from the new one in terms of product and service?
  5 It might be an idea to try to negotiate with the owner or look for new premises.

Pronunciation 1

  1 What <u>was</u> the name <u>of</u> the restaurant?
  2 If I <u>were</u> you, I'd look <u>for a</u> new office.
  3 <u>We're</u> going <u>to</u> look <u>at</u> the strengths, weaknesses, opportunities <u>and</u> threats.
  4 Some customers <u>can</u> sit outside.
  5 We <u>should</u> definitely think <u>about</u> starting <u>a</u> website <u>so</u> customers <u>could</u> order food <u>and</u> drinks <u>at their</u> desks.

Unit 28

3 1 c 2 h 3 b

4 1 Thank you, but I was really hoping for … (appraisal 1)
  2 We'd like to offer you … (appraisal 1)
  3 How about if we … (appraisal 2)
  4 You say that … (appraisal 2)
  5 That's right. (appraisal 2)
     That sounds great. (appraisal 2)
  6 I'm afraid that … (appraisal 3)
     I'm sorry, but … (appraisal 3)

Pronunciation 1

bis~~c~~uit business ca~~l~~m deb~~t~~ g~~u~~est g~~u~~ide hig~~h~~
~~h~~our is~~l~~and sig~~n~~ ve~~h~~icle ~~W~~ednesday w~~h~~ole woul~~d~~

5 1 I 2 I 3 I 4 E 5 I 6 E 7 I 8 I 9 E 10 E
11 E 12 E

Unit 29

1 That a high turnover does not necessarily mean high profits.

2 There are many reasons for this, but the main one is cashflow.

Pronunciation 1
1 These figures show‿earnings for the first six months.
2 Do‿I have to sign here?
3 Go to‿our homepage to find the link to the accounts.
4 I wanted to‿ask you‿about the overheads.
5 See you‿again soon.

3 1 Revenue / Income from sales   2 direct   3 gross
4 operating profit   5 indirect   6 net profit   7 return/ROI

5 1 300,000   2 130,000   3 100,000   4 270,000
5 30,000   6 3,000

6 *Suggested answer*
Look at why costs have risen so much without increasing turnover. Materials, salaries, consultancy fees, rent and fuel have all increased significantly.

Unit 30

1 1 f   2 h   3 g   4 b   5 a   6 e   7 d   8 c

3 1 T   2 T   3 T   4 F (She is a 'Wanderer' type.)   5 F (There have been repeated complaints.)   6 F (It has a warranty of three years.)   7 T

4 Good afternoon, everybody.
Does everyone have a copy of the agenda?
I'd like to aim for a (three o'clock) finish.
The most urgent matter is …
Can we go round the table on this?
Let's move on to the next point on the agenda.
I suggest we deal with that at next week's meeting.
(Cathy), I want you to …
(Takumi), you're going to …
(Kurt), it's your job to …

Unit 31

1 1 HR   2 RA   3 HR   4 RA   5 RA   6 HR

3 1 He makes sure that AON employs the most suitable people for the available positions in the Risk Assessment sector.
2 Recruitment agencies and on the company's website
3 To decide which candidates have suitable skills, as well as the necessary experience and knowledge for the position
4 Three
5 At least two department managers
6 Two from: salary, company benefits (e.g. private pension, healthcare, car, etc.), holiday entitlements

4 1 Advertise the job.
3 Telephone interview
5 Second onsite interview with HR
7 Negotiate terms of contract

Unit 32

1 *Suggested answers*
2 The world's population is growing and is going to continue to grow fast.
3 The BRICS countries' economies are growing quickly. China and India in particular will supply more of the world's goods and services.
4 The markets for tablets and mobile phones are growing globally. The market for PCs is declining. Mobile phones and tablets will be used more and more in the future.
5 An increasing number of customers are choosing to buy online. Customers will go out shopping less in the future.
6 The population is ageing, with the number of people over the age of 65 increasing all the time. In some parts of the world, the number of old people is going to double over the next 50 years..

3 communications, increasing global population, ageing population, BRICS

4 2, 3, 4, 5, 6

5 1 'll   2 aren't going to   3 bound   4 might not   5 likely
6 might   7 are going to   8 might

Pronunciation 1
1 I won't go.
2 They want to come.
3 You won't do it.
4 We want to pay the bill.

Pronunciation 3
1 I'll go.
2 We'll help you.
3 You work hard.
4 They'll play golf.

Unit 33

2 1 Themselves, the staff and the guests; the building; essential services (water, electricity); the computer system.
2 Flooding; fire; problems with the food (food poisoning); no guests; a breakdown in services (power cut); noise (construction of office block); crime (including vandalism and murder); nuclear attack
3 In case of a flood, they'd evacuate the hotel and move people to a safe place (another hotel on higher ground). They also suggest speaking to the local authorities, the council and the Environment Agency about taking precautions to protect the building.

3 1 f   2 c   3 a   4 b   5 d   6 e   7 h   8 g

Pronunciation 1
1 If there was a flood, we'd need to evacuate the hotel.
2 If a customer didn't pay, I'd speak to them first.
3 If we're late, we'll have to take a taxi.
4 If you call me tomorrow, I'll tell you the details.

Unit 34

3 Why did you move your production centre?
Which location did you choose?
Why did you choose Tunisia?
So will you move all your business to Tunisia in the future?

4 1 T   2 F (They built a new plant.)   3 F (The labour costs in Europe are more expensive.)   4 T   5 T

Pronunciation 1

/juː/	/uː/	/ə/
consume	fruit	focus
educated	include	supply
manufacture	juice	support
produce	June	
Tunisia	rule	
usual		

5 1 third   2 global   3 Geopolitical   4 provider
5 professionals   6 in-house

6

Benefits	Drawbacks
Lower costs	Reliance on third parties
Work done faster through a global workforce	Redundancies and demotivation caused by transferring jobs to other countries
Specialised skills	Geopolitical risks
Better availability of skilled professionals	Language differences and poor communication
Flexible labour	Lack of client focus from outsourcing provider
Cost efficiencies	Lack of in-house knowledge for business operations

Unit 35

1 **Primary:** 1 (farming), 6 (fishing), 10 (energy (renewables)), 12 (mining)
Secondary: 2 (manufacturing), 3 (construction), 11 (food processing)
Tertiary: 4 (police), 5 (banking), 7 (hospitality), 8 (tourism), 9 (nursing)

3 Yes, he does paint a positive picture, as Australia's economy is growing, unemployment is relatively low and the country is rich in natural resources.

4 1 T   2 F (The rate of unemployment is higher: 5.8%.)
3 T   4 T   5 F (Manufacturing is half what it was in the 1960s.)
6 F (Finance and tourism are the largest parts of the services sector.)

5 1 imports and exports   2 public spending   3 currency
4 commodities   5 rate of unemployment   6 renewables
7 gross domestic product (GDP)   8 rate of inflation

Pronunciation 1

oO	Oo
export (v)	export (n)
increase (v)	increase (n)
import (v)	import (n)

Pronunciation 2

oOo	oOoo	Ooo
employment	commodities	government
percentage	economy	industry

Unit 36

1 *Suggested answers*
Factories produce chemical, air and noise pollution.
Air travel produces climate-change gases and noise.
Nuclear power plants carry the risk of radioactive leaks, waste and water contamination.
Deforestation causes climate change and loss of habitat for animal species.
Shipping causes water pollution from oil and other waste.
Burning coal pollutes the air and causes climate change.

3 1 share cars   2 recycle waste   3 turn off water   4 avoid wasting paper   5 use 'green' transport   6 control office heating/cooling   7 buy locally

4 6, 5, 4, 7, 1

5 1 They can cut costs and improve the company's reputation.
2 Sensors that switch off lights automatically if there is no one in the room.
3 They could get benefits such as a dedicated parking space.

Unit 37

3 1 ('I don't know any other stores or products like these.')
3 ('... customers wanted something more, something different.')
5 ('Mr and Mrs Constantine understood the competition ...')
6 ('... the service is excellent. (I don't know any other stores or products like these.)')

4 1 T   2 F (They just look good enough to eat and are displayed like cheese.)   3 F (They hand out their catalogue in store when you buy something.)   4 F (They're pretty high.)
5 (They decided to do something different.)

5 1 b   2 f   3 c   4 g   5 a   6 d   7 e

Pronunciation 1
There are 16 schwa sounds.
1 Their price is the same as ours.
2 The atmosphere is warmer and more welcoming than other shops.
3 Lush is very different from its competitors.
4 Our costs aren't as high as theirs.
5 Their market share is bigger than ours.

6 *Suggested answers*
2 8 pm is earlier than 10 pm. Midnight is the latest.
3 The Republic of Korea has a smaller population than Japan. China has the biggest population.
4 Whisky is more expensive than wine. Beer is the cheapest.
5 Lufthansa carries more passengers than Qantas. Ryanair carries the most passengers.
6 A taxi is faster than a bicycle. A train is the fastest.
7 A mobile phone is more portable than a laptop computer. A desktop computer is the least portable.
8 Google is older than Bing. Yahoo! is the oldest.
9 Nuclear energy is better for the environment than fossil-fuel energy. Solar energy is the best for the environment.

Unit 38

3 1 A   2 A   3 B   4 B   5 B

Unit 39

3 1 Project Manager of a website   2 The Hague (Netherlands)   3 Seoul (Republic of Korea)   4 Brisbane (Australia)   5 instant messaging   6 data conferencing   7 face-to-face   8 Head of Product Forecasting   9 Singapore   10 Kuala Lumpur   11 Jakarta   12 e-mail   13 phone calls   14 video-conference

4 1 f   2 c   3 g   4 b   5 e   6 a   7 d

Unit 40

2

	new price
Phonecom	150c
Fulchester Football Club	150c
Bridge Automobiles	100c
PH Pharmaceuticals	800c
Tower Insurance	240c
Palace Leisure	180c
PB Oil	1,350c

4

	new price
Fulchester Football Club	100c
Bridge Automobiles	40c
PB Oil	1,500c
Guilders	300c
Blue K Mines	100c
Rockit Recording	210c
BexBio	500c
Mediamix	150c

CD track list

CD 1		CD 2	
Track 1	Audio 1.1	Track 1	Audio 21.1
Track 2	Audio 1.2	Track 2	Audio 21.2
Track 3	Audio 2.1	Track 3	Audio 22.1
Track 4	Audio 2.2	Track 4	Audio 22.2
Track 5	Audio 3.1	Track 5	Audio 23.1
Track 6	Audio 3.2	Track 6	Audio 24.1
Track 7	Audio 4.1	Track 7	Audio 24.2
Track 8	Audio 4.2	Track 8	Audio 25.1
Track 9	Audio 4.3	Track 9	Audio 25.2
Track 10	Audio 5.1	Track 10	Audio 27.1
Track 11	Audio 5.2	Track 11	Audio 27.2
Track 12	Audio 6.1	Track 12	Audio 28.1
Track 13	Audio 6.2	Track 13	Audio 28.2
Track 14	Audio 7.1	Track 14	Audio 28.3
Track 15	Audio 8.1	Track 15	Audio 28.4
Track 16	Audio 8.2	Track 16	Audio 29.1
Track 17	Audio 8.3	Track 17	Audio 29.2
Track 18	Audio 9.1	Track 18	Audio 30.1
Track 19	Audio 10.1	Track 19	Audio 31.1
Track 20	Audio 10.2	Track 20	Audio 31.2
Track 21	Audio 11.1	Track 21	Audio 32.1
Track 22	Audio 12.1	Track 22	Audio 32.2
Track 23	Audio 12.2	Track 23	Audio 32.3
Track 24	Audio 13.1	Track 24	Audio 32.4
Track 25	Audio 14.1	Track 25	Audio 32.5
Track 26	Audio 14.2	Track 26	Audio 33.1
Track 27	Audio 15.1	Track 27	Audio 34.1
Track 28	Audio 15.2	Track 28	Audio 34.2
Track 29	Audio 16.1	Track 29	Audio 35.1
Track 30	Audio 16.2	Track 30	Audio 35.2
Track 31	Audio 16.3	Track 31	Audio 35.3
Track 32	Audio 17.1	Track 32	Audio 36.1
Track 33	Audio 18.1	Track 33	Audio 37.1
Track 34	Audio 18.2	Track 34	Audio 37.2
Track 35	Audio 18.3	Track 35	Audio 38.1
Track 36	Audio 18.4	Track 36	Audio 39.1
Track 37	Audio 19.1	Track 37	Audio 40.1
Track 38	Audio 19.2	Track 38	Audio 40.2
Track 39	Audio 20.1		
Track 40	Audio 20.2		

Teacher's feedback sheet

Use this page to monitor students' speaking performances and provide them with feedback.

Grammar	Vocabulary	Functions and expressions	Pronunciation

Photocopiable © Delta Publishing Ltd 2015